99-542-61

LOVE IN THE NBA

STAN LOVE & RON RAPOPORT

New York

LOVE IN THE NBA

A Player's Uninhibited Diary

Saturday Review Press / E. P. Dutton & Co., Inc.

Library of Congress Cataloging in Publication Data

Love, Stan.
Love in the NBA.

1. Love, Stan. 2. National Basketball Association.
3. Basketball. I. Rapoport, Ron, joint author. II. Title.
GV884.L68A34 1975   796.32'3'0924 [B] 75-23499

Published simultaneously in Canada by Clarke, Irwin & Company
Limited,
Toronto and Vancouver
ISBN: 0-8415-0398-2
Designed by The Etheredges

For my mother and father
With love and gratitude

ACKNOWLEDGMENTS

At various times during the preparation of this book, the explanatory skills of Cheryl Van Blaricom and Steve Love were put to the severest of tests. It is hereby confirmed officially that all those tests were passed *summa cum laude*. In addition, Richard Levin's coverage of the Lakers in the Los Angeles *Herald-Examiner* proved valuable in untangling dates and events that, because of the hectic nature of the NBA schedule, often came and went faster than taping sessions did.

And to Sara Keith, who transcribed our voices from amidst a background of rolling waves, varooming motorcycles, ringing telephones, clattering pots and pans, and a wide variety of competing sounds in general: bless you for your skill and patience.

LOVE IN THE NBA

PREFACE: A DUET

AUGUST 20

To be completely truthful, the subtitle of this book should probably be "A Player's Uninhibited Half-Diary." Our plan, as unorthodox as it may be, is to write about the 1974–1975 National Basketball Association season from this date until the All-Star break in the third week of January. There are several reasons for this and it seems reasonable to get them out front before beginning.

First—and this may be heresy for a professional athlete contemplating a new season—it is less than certain that it will all end in the final seconds of the seventh game of the last round of the playoffs with Stan Love stealing the ball from Dave Cowens, driving the length of the court, and sinking a shot from the corner to give Los Angeles the NBA championship. The Lakers appear to be an interesting team from this perspective but perhaps less than a championship one. Stan's own prospects are equally ill-defined at this moment.

Second, that is not the book we want to write anyway. What we have in mind is a look at what it's like to play professional basketball in the United States in the mid-1970s: the pleasures, the problems, the pressures, the players, the coaches, the front office, and so on. In short, the whole NBA experience. For this, it does not seem necessary to go through an 82-game season (not counting exhibition games or the playoffs) that won't end until June. Between the opening of practice in September and the All-Star break some four months later, the Lakers will play every team in the league, visit almost every city, and, with any luck at all, encounter every situation attendant to pro basketball at this point in time. The diary form, in essence, is simply a device to bring Stan's perceptions to bear on his corner of the sporting world. There is no reason to drag it out unnecessarily. When the season does end, we plan a short epilogue to tie up any loose ends that have been unraveled in the course of the journey.

Here, then, is Stan Love's half-diary, in which the "we" of these few lines will be abandoned. From now on, Stan speaks for himself.

AUGUST 27

The season begins on the beach. It is early in the morning, hours before the bikinis and the bicycles arrive, and we are running in the hard sand near the water. Our goal is a pier two miles from my house in Manhattan Beach, which is half a block from the water. When we get there, we'll rest a few minutes and then run back. Running with me is Ron, a schoolteacher friend who has his summers free. When we've finished running, we'll go to the gym and lift weights, then shoot some baskets, play paddleball, and take a sauna. Allowing a little time to eat and a little time to rest, this will take us into the late afternoon, when we will finally quit, exhausted.

Except for a trip to Japan I took with some other pro basketball players earlier this month, we've been doing this almost every day for two months now and I can see the results. When we first started, I couldn't get to the pier without stopping. Now I can run the four miles at a pretty decent speed with just a little break. Give me the three more weeks before practice starts and I'll be in the best shape of my life.

I pay Ron $50 a day to work out with me. I know that sounds crazy, but there's a good reason for it: I'm lazy. So lazy, in fact, that if Ron didn't ring my doorbell at eight o'clock every morning, I'd just turn over and go back to sleep. Then, when I did get up, I'd find an excuse not to run. The beach would be too crowded or the sun would be too hot or some muscle would be aching. But I know I have to work out. So I give Ron the $50 and he gets me up and we run.

Except for a few dedicated surfers—guys in the head-to-toe wet suits that ward off the cold—we are the only ones around. But somehow it always seems as if there is plenty of company. It's only in my head, but that doesn't make it any the less real. There's Happy Hairston and Connie Hawkins and Bill Bridges and Pat Riley. And up over the horizon I think I see Cazzie Russell. They are the other Laker forwards. My teammates. My friends. My enemies. They are the ones I have to compete with if I'm going to do any real playing this year. That's why it seems as if they're with me wherever I go.

Frankly, I feel that I have a shot at them this year. Hairston is 32 now—seven years older than I am—and has had some injuries. He came back strong last year, but I don't think they're counting on him to play quite as much this year. Hawkins is also 32 and sometimes he looks as good as he ever was —which may be as good as anybody has ever been—but not consistently. He averaged only 12.6 points a game last year. Bridges is 35 and was strictly a substitute in defensive situa-

3

tions last year. Riley is 29 and plays some forward but generally comes off the bench as a guard. That leaves Kermit Washington, the Lakers' top draft choice last season. He spent the whole year on the bench; his knees are in pretty bad shape—he's been taking acupuncture treatments—and I think they like him as a center anyhow. And Seymour Reed, a rookie from Bradley, who's supposed to be a gunner but has to be a long shot. And Cazzie Russell.

It looks more and more like we're going to get him. He's played out his option with the Golden State Warriors and keeps saying that he wants to play in Los Angeles. The Lakers would be out of their minds not to try to get him, of course, because he's one of the best shooting forwards in the league. He averaged 20.5 points a game last year, and you can't be negative about having a guy of that caliber on your team. Can you?

But I'm optimistic. I really am. I just wish practice would start so I can be done with this damn running.

AUGUST 31

I think a transformation has taken place in Stan's attitude since the end of the season and I think you will be favorably impressed with his more serious and businesslike demeanor.

Well, there it is. The first assault on public enemy number one—my image. It's part of a letter my brother Steve, who is also my business manager, sent today to Pete Newell, the Lakers' general manager. Steve and I have talked a lot this summer about why I haven't been able to accomplish what

I've wanted to in my three years in the NBA, which is to play regularly, to contribute, to be a real part of the team. I know that I have the talent, that my basic skills, especially my scoring potential, can be as good as any forward's on the team if I can just get a chance to develop them. But I haven't been able to achieve that status where you get a steady amount of playing time, where you are a key factor on the team. It's really very frustrating.

Part of the problem may have been something I haven't had any control over. When I came out of the University of Oregon as the first draft choice of the Baltimore Bullets in 1971, I was a center. That was all I had ever played. But it was clear from the beginning that I was going to have to be a forward in the NBA. At 6-9 and 210 (the NBA guide lists me at 215, but that's only wishful thinking), I simply wasn't big enough to compete underneath with Kareem Abdul-Jabbar or Wilt Chamberlain. Besides, the Bullets already had Wes Unseld, who had been second in rebounding only to Chamberlain the season before and would be again. So that meant I had to make two big adjustments: from college to the pros and from center to forward. It wasn't easy, and I'm the first to admit that I never really made the transition the way I'd hoped I could. Or the way the Bullets had hoped.

But there's something else that has been aggravating the situation and it's taken a while for me to realize it. It's the way I am perceived, my image: tall, skinny, kind of gawky with a lot of wild curly blond hair and a droopy mustache. Likes to kid around a lot, doesn't always take things too seriously. Born and bred in Southern California. Brother of one of the Beach Boys, who for a decade have spoken to an entire generation of American kids. Single, lives in a house on the beach, wears a lot of tank tops and tie-dyed shirts and cutoff jeans. In short, a flake.

Lately I've begun to see how it puts me in this cozy little pigeonhole that makes it easy for people to label me, to "understand" me. Now I suppose it's all right to be a little out of the ordinary if you're a great star—Walt Frazier and his kinky clothes, Wilt Chamberlain and his million-dollar house—and it certainly didn't affect the way I was thought of as a basketball player in college. At Oregon I was an All-American, the leading scorer in the conference, the holder of most of the school scoring records, and oh, yes, something of a flake.

But when you are struggling to make it, things are different. The way people see you off the court begins to affect their judgments of you on it. Judgments by the front office and coaches, by the press and fans, even by your teammates to some extent. The logic is this: "A good basketball player is one who takes the game seriously. A flake is somebody who doesn't take the game seriously. Therefore . . ."

And after a while everything written and said publicly about you is calculated to press you into that mold, to reconfirm your public image. An example of this comes to mind right away. Last year a reporter for a local paper did a story about me for the Laker program. Now nobody ever writes about me without mentioning what I look like, where I live, and who my brother Mike is. In fact, the title of this story was "A Free Spirit."

In it the writer told of a time when I was at Oregon and a few of us made an impromptu appearance in a canoe at an annual riverfront festival, which was held before about 5,000 spectators on Mother's Day. Much of the story was true—we did come paddling along in the middle of all the floats and create a bit of an uproar. But the writer couldn't resist adding one little detail—that my friends and I were in the nude on the occasion. The truth is we weren't, and I have newspaper pictures to prove it. But with just a few creative taps on the typewriter, the addition of half a dozen words, he was able to turn an item about a bunch of college kids who'd drunk a little beer and had a little fun into another freaky Stan Love story. After a while your image can become more real to people than the facts.

None of this ever really bothered me until I saw it affecting my career. Once last season some friends told me that Chick Hearn, the Lakers' broadcaster, had angrily said on the air that I was laughing on the bench while we were losing a game. That may not sound important, but Chick is a vice president of the club and very influential. He is the most accurate reflection there is of a player's status on the team and is crucial in establishing your image. When I heard about what he had said, I figured I'd better try to find out what was going on, so I asked Pete Newell about it. It turned out that laughing instead of frowning was the least of it.

Newell said there were reports that I was breaking training and not taping my ankles before games. He also said there was a rumor that I wasn't playing aggressively against the black players on other teams. It was so ridiculous—such crazy, foolish nonsense—that I couldn't believe it. For the first time I knew I was in bad trouble.

Steve's letter to Newell is the beginning of our campaign to try to turn things around. We figure that Pete may be sympathetic to my situation because he was responsible for my acquisition from Baltimore last season. He wants to see me succeed not only because of my ballplaying potential, but also because it might reflect poorly on his judgment to have traded for a high-priced ballplayer who didn't work out.

Before the season starts Steve and I want to have a meeting with Bill Sharman, the Lakers' coach, to tell him how serious I am. I really always have been, but if I have to actively convince people of it, then I will try to convince people. So get ready for the new Stan Love, sports fans. I just hope it isn't too late.

SEPTEMBER 2

I have been looking through *Ball Four* and *Instant Replay* to try to pick up a few pointers on how to write a best-selling sports diary, and I see that very early in both books there is a discussion of money. Both Jim Bouton and Jerry Kramer tell these terrible stories of how cheap and devious management is and how you have to stand up and demand what you're worth or you'll get screwed every time. Bouton's attitude is one of bitterness, while Kramer's seems more to be, "That's the way it is and what can you do about it?" I'm sure that's the way things are in baseball and football, but my own feelings on the subject are a little different. I mean, it's tough for me to put down a sport that pays me an annual salary well into six figures.

I know a lot of people think it's ridiculous for us to get that kind of money for what we do and, in a sense, maybe it is. Steve and I have talked about it and we are both concerned about the ability of the teams to keep paying such enormous salaries and stay in business. But if you look at it another way, perhaps what we make isn't that much out of line after all.

Let's say that half the men in the United States have played some form of basketball—in school or on the playgrounds—when they were young. That seems like a conservative estimate to me: maybe 60 million people. There are 17 teams in the NBA with 12 players each. That's 204 players. Throw in the ABA and you wind up with about 300. In other words, for every 20,000 men who have played basketball, only one develops the necessary skills to play with the country's top professionals. Now, let's relate that to almost any other competitive line of work. What do the top 300 corporate executives in America make? A lot more than the $90,000 or so we average in the NBA, right? Or, to take something a little closer to home, what does the top one-out-of-20,000 actor make? Or the top rock musician? The answer, of course, is that a Robert Redford or a Bob Dylan takes home more than twice as much as a Kareem Abdul-Jabbar and nobody thinks a thing of it.

And if you really consider it, we're in the same line of work they are. We're part of the performing arts, too. Our act is out there in front of the public just as much as movies or television or concerts are. We're competing for the same entertainment dollar and I don't think it's unreasonable for us to be paid on the same scale once we've reached the top and all

8

the guys who didn't make it have fallen by the wayside.

There's something else to consider, too. Public tastes change, of course, but the top show business personalities go on forever. Paul Newman can keep acting until he drops or decides he's had enough. The Beach Boys are already performing to a whole new generation of kids and with greater success than ever. But the average life of a professional athlete is four or five years. If a basketball player can hang on for eight or ten years, he's doing great. But one day—and one day soon —it's all going to end. Your legs give out, your shooting eye isn't what it once was and it's good-by to the big money. The skills you've spent your whole life developing suddenly aren't worth a dime and at the age of 30 or so—which is when most people are just beginning to hit their stride—you find yourself obsolete. So you'd better have put some of the money you were making aside or you'll face a drastic change in your lifestyle. It's something every professional athlete I know worries about, no matter how much money he's making at any given moment.

Actually, the money I'm getting isn't all that much for a first-round draft choice compared to some of the salaries and bonuses that are being paid now. When I read about some of these huge contracts, though, I have to wonder if the players are really getting paid that much. A lot of those figures could be inflated for several reasons.

Say somebody signs for a million dollars. Part of the contract might call for payments of $10,000 a year from age 40 to 65, which is $250,000. But when you consider today's rate of inflation, plus the interest that money can earn for the team between the time the contract is signed and the time it is paid out, that $250,000 might be worth only $80,000 today. There are tax advantages to deferment, of course, but basically the longer the money is deferred, the less the contract is really worth.

When Steve and I first started negotiating with the Bullets, they offered something like $50,000 for the first five years, $30,000 for the next five years, then $25,000, and so on. We said, "No way." If I was supposed to get $25,000 in 1984, that might be worth only $10,000 in terms of 1971 dollars. We finally did settle on a deferred contract—a four-year deal payable over six years. Deferred, in other words, but not for very long.

There is, of course, one major reason why salaries in the NBA are so high. And that is the ABA. Happy Hairston said that when he broke into the league ten years ago he signed for $9,000. The next year he got $12,500, then $15,000, then $20,000. It wasn't until after the ABA was organized that he finally made the breakthrough into the big money. But now, with the two leagues bidding for the relatively small number of name players who come out of colleges every year, the players are put in a very strong bargaining position. In fact, it's very difficult to determine your market value as a ballplayer when you read about all the million-dollar contracts guys are supposed to be getting. You try to figure out what your relative worth might be to a team in need of your talents.

In 1971 I was drafted by the Dallas Chaparrals of the ABA as well as by the NBA Bullets. Steve and an agent named Nicholas Grillo, who was managing the Beach Boys at the time, did all the contract bargaining. We asked both teams for $750,000 over five years. Abe Pollin, the Bullets' owner, came back with an offer of $300,000 and said that was it, his one and only offer. He was not going to get into a bidding war with the ABA, he said. Dallas came in at around $400,000. I didn't get involved in the negotiations until the end, when I chose between the final offers.

One of the attractive features of the Dallas offer was a bonus of $50,000 just for signing. They also threw in free rent anywhere I wanted to live in Dallas and a car. In addition, the Chaparrals agreed to buy insurance policies that would have paid the full amount of the contract in case I became injured and couldn't play. Baltimore refused to do that. Pollin was adamant: if you couldn't play, you didn't get paid. But one problem we saw was that the ABA was in worse shape financially than the NBA. We were concerned about what would happen if the league or the Chaparrals folded. So Steve and Nick wanted the Dallas owner, Bob Folsom, to guarantee the contract personally.

10

Eventually, we came to an agreement with Dallas on everything but that final point—guaranteeing the contract—and we flew to Dallas to complete negotiations. The club put out a story that I was coming to sign a contract, and as soon as our plane touched down we were hustled into one of the airline's VIP rooms, where there were television cameras, microphones, and newspaper reporters waiting.

While Steve and Nick continued the negotiations, I went on a tour of Dallas with the Chaparral broadcaster, Terry Stembridge. I had no idea what was happening until I met Steve for lunch and he said, "Come on, we're going to Baltimore." Folsom still wouldn't agree to guarantee the contract. In the meantime, the Bullets had heard the story that I was about to sign with Dallas and they frantically called Steve to ask if it was true or if we were still open to negotiations. Steve said we were ready to listen if they were ready to talk about significantly more dollars. So we flew to Baltimore to meet with Pollin again.

The Bullets' office is in downtown Baltimore, and to get there from the airport we had to drive past some of the worst slums I've ever seen. I wondered what I was getting into, whether I knew what I was doing. Dallas was a beautiful city by comparison. The contrast was like going from Harlem to Beverly Hills. Pollin increased his offer for a four-year contract and he offered his personal guarantee. That is something he'd never given before and as a matter of fact it wasn't all that important to us as far as the Bullets were concerned. We figured the NBA wasn't in any immediate danger of folding. Still, it was a nice gesture on Abe's part.

While we were still talking to the Bullets, the Chaparrals called one last time and offered to guarantee *half* the contract. That seemed a little strange to us, but the Dallas offer was over $100,000 more than Baltimore's final offer and Steve and Nick finally recommended that I sign with Dallas. In the end, my choice was not based entirely on financial considerations.

While we were in Baltimore, the Bullets were in the middle of the playoffs with Milwaukee and I went out to see one of the games. It was very impressive watching Kareem Abdul-

Jabbar and the Bucks play Baltimore. Somehow the whole aura of the NBA was just more appealing than the ABA. All this talk about money was exciting, but it was so unrealistic. Here we were talking about what seemed to be such huge amounts of money and I had been living on $125 a month at college. I just couldn't totally relate to it. The NBA was a better league and had the better players. That's why I signed with Baltimore.

SEPTEMBER 4

During my first season with the Bullets we were in Atlanta and Rich Rinaldi and I decided to get a look at the Regency Hyatt House, that futuristic new hotel, and have lunch there. We sat at a table next to a couple with five or six kids, which reminded me a little of my own large family—two brothers, three sisters. It's kind of hard to hide the fact that you're a basketball player when you're out in public—you can't walk around all hunched over—and it turned out that they were big fans and were going to see us play the Hawks that night. So we signed autographs, kidded around, and took their pictures for them.

Our waitress, a slender brunette with a sensational smile, seemed to be enjoying the situation as much as we were. Her name tag said Cheryl. When the talk got around to basketball, she said she'd seen only a couple of games in her life and none since she'd been in high school. Well, I certainly know an opening when I see one, so I invited her to come to the game that night.

"No, no, I have other things to do," she said. But then I got an assist from the man with all those kids.

"They're really very nice guys," he said. "You don't have

to worry at all. If you like, you can sit with us." I couldn't have been more grateful to him.

But Cheryl wasn't convinced and disappeared into the bar, where she started folding napkins. Now I'm not the sort of person who chases waitresses all over restaurants, but she seemed so nice, not at all uptight, that I just had to follow her into that bar.

"Can I help you fold those napkins?" I asked her. (Warren Beatty could learn a lot from me.) She just laughed. We continued our conversation and finally she agreed that I could leave her a ticket for the game.

It turned out to be a very close, exciting game with the Hawks, and afterward I asked her if she'd enjoyed it.

"Well, it was nice watching you play," she said.

"But I was only in for 15 or 20 minutes," I said. "What about the game? Didn't you see how close the score was?"

Finally, she admitted she hadn't even noticed there was a scoreboard. It was beginning to dawn on me that this was an unusual girl. She certainly wasn't interested in me because I was a basketball player.

There was no whirlwind courtship after that because the Bullets didn't get back to Atlanta for a couple of months. But when we did, I always ended up at the Regency Hyatt House and Cheryl always ended up at the basketball game. I would have preferred a little more variety in the places we went, but my evenings were pretty much spoken for. About all I could ask her was whether she wanted to see the Bullets shoot down the Hawks.

That summer Cheryl went to Europe for several months and we wrote to each other a lot. When she got back, I convinced her to come out to California to visit. It was the first time we'd been together for more than a day or two—as Cheryl puts it, we'd never spent enough time together to be on anything more than good behavior.

The next season we saw each other about once a month. She came up to Baltimore several times and out to my permanent home in Los Angeles a couple of times that summer. It seemed as if all the money she was making was spent on plane

13

fares—either to Baltimore or to California. We talked about her moving to Baltimore, but before we decided anything I was traded to the Lakers. So she put all her stuff in her Volkswagen and drove out to Los Angeles alone, without even a radio in her car. I said she was an unusual girl.

SEPTEMBER 6

Steve and I finally met with Bill Sharman today. We'd been trying to get together with him earlier in the summer to see if we could find out what his plans are for my role on the team this season. But he always seemed to be away at the boys' basketball camp he runs in San Diego or with his wife, who has been very sick for a long time. So we never really pressed it.

I did see Bill at his camp when I went there one day to be an instructor. Driving down, I wondered if I'd be able to slide into a conversation with him about where I stand, but it wasn't a very good place for it. Whenever we talked, a dozen kids stood around listening.

One boy asked Bill if we were getting a guard—I forget who—from another NBA team and he said we weren't.

"Well, are you getting Cazzie Russell?" the boy asked.

"We don't know yet," Bill said.

"Guards are OK," I said. "Forwards no."

We all just laughed.

I guess the most important thing Steve and I wanted to accomplish in our meeting with Bill today was to allay any fears he might have about my "attitude" problem.

"I'm ready to play," I told him. "I've been working out hard all summer. All I want is a chance to contribute."

"I'm really happy to hear that," he said. "There was a time

14

when I was concerned that you weren't taking things seriously enough. But the last half of last season I was really pleased to see that your attitude was positive. You know, you're one of the ballplayers on the team that I like, and I've got to admit that I don't like everybody."

Steve and I laughed at that, and I stifled my impulse to ask him which players he didn't like. Bill then said he hadn't been happy with our front-line play last year.

"Does that mean that all the positions are wide open?" I asked.

"Everything is going to be open and fair," he said. "I don't care if a guy is a ten-year veteran. If he doesn't produce—well, nobody's got a position nailed down."

Then he said he knew what my situation was and that maybe it wasn't really all my fault.

"Some players get drafted out of college to teams where they really aren't needed," he said. "And other guys get sent to teams where they can walk right in and play 20 to 25 minutes a game right away. I know when you were in Baltimore you were locked into a team that was set with its forwards."

He was right, of course. During my first season with Baltimore I played only what the Bullets considered to be token rookie-development time. They kept waiting for Gus Johnson to do all the tremendous things he used to be able to do when he was healthy; but by then his legs were gone. And the offense that Gene Shue, the Bullets' coach, liked to use had one big rebounding forward and one small running forward, almost a third guard. There was no way I could beat out the smaller guy, Mike Riordan; in a way, he wasn't even playing my position. Then, in my second season, the Bullets got Elvin Hayes, who was taller, heavier, stronger, and more experienced than I was. Also better.

But one of the problems that concerns me now is that the same thing might be happening all over again with the Lakers. The fact that most of the forwards are in their thirties can work in my favor, but it also makes them experienced veterans, and with the Lakers that's important. Los Angeles is not the kind of team that can take the time to develop players, to let them get experience. They have to win this year and every year. In a way, it's safer in such a situation to go with the veterans.

Say we're losing with Connie Hawkins and Happy Hairston playing up front. Nobody can blame the coach because he's using the guys who have been around, who know the opposing players and who have an established record. All people can say is, "Well, he's playing his stars and they just aren't producing." But if we lose with me in there, people can easily say, "Why the hell is he playing Love? Where are Hawkins and Hairston?"

One thing I've learned is that everybody faces his own pressures, no matter how good his situation might appear. In a way, Bill's job is in jeopardy as much as mine or anybody else's. If he doesn't produce for the Lakers, he's gone. Bill has won championships in every league he's coached in. Three years ago, during the 1971–1972 season, the Lakers won 69 of the 82 games they played, an all-time NBA record. They also won 33 in a row that year, which is not only a record but one of the most amazing feats in sports history. Bill just has an unbelievable record, and it's hard to think in terms of his having to prove himself.

While we were talking to Bill, a secretary called and said that Jack Kent Cooke, the owner of the Lakers, wanted to see Bill in his office right away. That ended the meeting immediately, of course, and as we went out the door we saw everybody scurrying toward Cooke's office—Pete Newell, Chick Hearn, and Larry Creger, the new head of player personnel. It was interesting to watch. The owner of the team calls his troops and they drop what they're doing and come running. But even as we were walking out the door, Bill was talking to me, telling me what to work on.

"Try to go to a gym and play against an imaginary defender," he said, and he started dribbling a make-believe basketball and making moves on a make-believe player as he headed toward Cooke's office. "Keep low on defense. Sustain your running power. Work on your quickness."

16

Steve was impressed that Bill would be trying to help me even while he was on his way to a meeting with his boss. And I think we both came away feeling we'd accomplished something. I got the impression that the Lakers really do want me to succeed and that I will get an honest chance this season. And that, I guess, is all I can ask for.

The big meeting in Cooke's office didn't last very long. In a few minutes they all went over to the Forum Club to hold a press conference. The Lakers had just signed Cazzie Russell.

SEPTEMBER 8

Dorothy Sharman died yesterday. She was a young and beautiful and vibrant woman and I wish I'd gotten to know her better. It was cancer, the kind that drags on and on while you run around looking for miracles: going to all the hospitals, seeing all the specialists, taking all the treatments. None of which does much good.

Her illness completely devastated Bill; last season it seemed as if he was gone from the team almost as much as he was with it. Even when he was there, you could see that he was under pressure, that he wasn't completely devoted to the team the way he had been. How could he be?

Bill didn't talk about it much, only to say Dorothy was in or out of the hospital again. After a while he didn't say anything at all. If you asked how she was, just to let him know you were thinking of her, he'd say, "She has some good days and some bad ones."

As far as the team was concerned, it may have been a little disconcerting to have him coming and going so much—John Barnhill, the assistant coach, took over when he was gone—

but in a way it might have had a unifying effect too. We never held any Knute Rockne kind of meetings—no "Let's win one for the coach." It was a completely unspoken thing. But I think the guys may have put out a little more because of it.

A lot of people thought last season was Bill's finest coaching job. The Lakers had lost Wilt Chamberlain and had traded Jim McMillian; Jerry West was injured most of the year. We were down in the standings, and Golden State was doing so well for a while that it looked as if we might not make the playoffs. But we came on strong at the end and won the division title. It was said that Bill really met the challenge by pulling the right strings on a team that wasn't all that strong.

Well, I think it was his greatest performance as a coach too, but not because of the way he ran the team or his basketball strategy. Just leaving the team for those long flights to be with Dorothy, then flying back to tell a bunch of guys how to bounce and pass and shoot a big round ball—that's what showed me the kind of man Bill Sharman is.

SEPTEMBER 14

So much for hypnotism. And it sounded like such a good idea. Of course, I didn't have any illusions that a hypnotist would be able to improve my defense or my shooting percentage, but I had hoped he could use the power of suggestion to help me gain some weight and enjoy running on the beach a little more. Besides, I'd never been hypnotized and I'd always been curious about it.

I've been trying to gain weight ever since I was in high school, but it's been hopeless. I stopped growing when I was 16 and I weighed 205. Since then I've gained five pounds. And, believe me, I've tried everything: weight lifting, superprotein diet supplements, liquid nutriments, four meals a day, five meals a day, malts between meals, you name it. Once, at college, I almost got up to 220, but then the basketball season started and I came back down again.

Right now I eat three meals and two snacks a day, including a lot of fattening stuff, but I just don't gain. I guess it's my metabolism. Or nerves. One of the problems is I can't eat those huge meals a lot of athletes put away. It's amazing to watch some of these guys eat. Bill Bridges on the Lakers is a big eater; Wes Unseld of the Bullets used to just crush the food. I understand Wilt Chamberlain could drink half a gallon of orange juice at one sitting. But I eat until I get full and then I stop. It's uncomfortable for me to keep eating.

As far as running is concerned, I've never liked it. I mean to the point where I'd get through and say, "Out of sight. Let's run two more miles." I'd like to get over the desire to stop when I'm physically and mentally tired, just when it does the most good. It would be a tremendous help, I think, to be able to go on when I want to quit.

Anyway, my brother Mike put me in touch with a hypnotist in Hollywood who said he could use the power of suggestion to help me gain weight. He said I'd eat more, and more often. Also, I'd relax more and not burn up the food so fast. But the appointment today was disappointing. First, the hypnotist's office looked like a Goodwill collection store—it didn't inspire a lot of confidence. We talked for a while and then he hypnotized me, but I don't think I took it very well. My arms and legs felt heavy and I got numb and relaxed, but I don't think it was effective.

"How relaxed do you feel?" he said. "Rate how you feel on a scale of 1 to 30."

"About 15," I said. "Halfway, I guess."

Actually, the feeling I had was somewhat similar to the sensation I get when I meditate, which my brother Mike turned me on to. I've been meditating on and off for a couple of years, although it's been mostly off. To do it properly, you should really meditate twice a day, once in the morning just after you get up and then again in the evening. My problem is that I like to eat as soon as I get up, and you can't meditate on a full stomach. It's lack of discipline on my part.

The only time I can really get into it is when the team is traveling. When we're on the plane, I'll close my eyes and meditate. I guess everybody thinks I'm sleeping. It completely relaxes me, makes me feel like I've had a couple of drinks. When I come out of it, I'm very sensitive to my surroundings. Everything seems a lot brighter and I feel well rested and calm. If you meditate regularly, this feeling is supposed to be with you all the time, increasing your level of perception and energy. Many scientific studies have verified this and I can understand why more and more athletes are getting into it, guys with very diverse personalities—from Joe Namath to Bill Walton.

So since the hypnotist didn't make me feel any different than the way I felt after meditating, I don't see any point in continuing with him. Or in paying him $15 a session.

SEPTEMBER 17

I took my Laker physical today. For the second time. A couple of days ago they tested my reflexes and listened to my heart, but when they said to go over to the hospital for a blood test, I got in my car and drove home. I have never liked needles and will go to great lengths to avoid any kind of shot. In college they learned not to schedule my flu shots until after I got to basketball practice. Then they would take all my clothes and not give them back to me until I'd had my shot.

Last year I got out of the blood test, but today they called and said I had to come in for it. While I was there, I had my back X-rayed. The pictures showed that my back is all screwed up, which is nothing new; it always has been. They think my right leg is longer than the left, and that something is wrong with the bone structure of my spine. I told the doctor looking at the X-rays to call Dr. Kerlan, who is familiar with my situation.

Robert Kerlan is one of the top orthopedists in the country and is into sports medicine in a big way. He's a consultant for the Lakers, Rams, Dodgers, the Strings of World Team Tennis, to name a few. Athletes from all over the country are sent to him when they have problems, and he also writes a national newspaper column called "The Sports Doctor."

But he has also been for years the Love family physician for everything that doesn't work right. My mother first took me to him when I broke my arm in grade school. After that I was in and out of his office—twice with a broken arm and a number of times for my back. In fact, it seemed like my mother always had one of us in there. We all had broken bones at one time or another, including my sister Stephanie, who broke a leg. Once Steve nearly cut off some toes, and another time Mike hurt his back. Usually, Dr. Kerlan saw mothers come in screaming hysterically because their kids had been hurt, but all Mom would say was, "Here's another one. Can you fix him up?" To this day, he says she should be mother of the year because she took our injuries so philosophically.

When I was in the seventh grade, I had a pinched nerve in my neck and Mom took me to Dr. Kerlan. I remember being very impressed by seeing a couple of the Lakers there. Gee, I thought, Elgin Baylor, Rudy LaRusso, and I all go to the same doctor. I was sitting on a table when Dr. Kerlan came in and asked what the problem was. I told him I had a pinched nerve and once in a while I had to hold my head in my hands because something would snap and none of the muscles in my neck would work.

So Dr. Kerlan grabbed my head and said, "Lean back. Relax. Relax. I'm not going to hurt you." He turned my head one way and then another, saying, "Does this hurt? Does that hurt?" I said no and he said to relax again. All of a sudden he twisted my head completely around. And I mean *completely*. I was looking over my left shoulder and I could see my right one. That scene in *The Exorcist* was nothing new to me. I lived it. The pain was so bad I could hardly believe it and I was sweating like I'd been playing ball for two hours. I swore at him and shouted that he was a liar, that he had said he wouldn't hurt me. He just ignored it and said my neck would be all right from then on. Which it has been.

When the doctor looking at the X-rays of my back called Dr. Kerlan, I could hear him say, "Put him on the phone."

"Yes, doctor," I said in my best patient-to-physician voice.

"Damn it, Stan," he said, "if you were disciplined and would come in for treatments once a week and do your stretching exercises, your back would get better."

I started to answer him, but he wouldn't listen. He called me a Communist and every terrible thing he could think of. I've gotten a lot of great medical attention from Dr. Kerlan over the years, but never any sympathy. Having him yell at me didn't make getting the shot any easier either.

SEPTEMBER 18

The Lakers held their first practice sessions at the Loyola University gym today and there were two surprises. The first was that Jack Kent Cooke was there. The second was that Gail Goodrich wasn't.

Cooke owns not only the Lakers but also the Kings of the National Hockey League, the Forum (where both teams play), and a large percentage of the Washington Redskins of the National Football League. He is also involved in a million other business deals, so even though he has an office in the Forum you rarely see him.

The first time I met him was just after the Lakers got me from the Bullets, and they brought me over to the Forum to introduce me around. Cooke has this big booming voice, and even when he's talking to somebody right next to him he comes on like Laurence Olivier reciting Shakespeare.

"Stan," he said as I walked into his office, "I can't tell you how happy we are that you're a Laker. We think you can become the best forward ever to play in Los Angeles. Do you believe that?"

I must have looked pretty silly standing there with my mouth open, but I finally managed to say something clever like, "Why . . . yes." I must admit, though, that I did wonder what Elgin Baylor would think.

Cooke was out of Los Angeles almost all of last season because TelePrompTer, which he also runs, was having financial problems. He moved to New York to try to bail it out. But now he's back and everybody knew he was at practice because of his voice. He talked to Bill Sharman and Pat Riley and Brian Winters, our rookie guard from South Carolina, and then he just hung around and watched us practice.

It wasn't until afterward, when I was in the locker room, that Frank O'Neill, our trainer, said, "Did you hear what happened to Cooke today?"

"No," I said. "What?"

"He got sued for $175 million by some TelePrompTer stockholders."

I walked back to the swinging doors that lead out to the floor of the gym and looked through the window at Cooke again, thinking about F. Scott Fitzgerald and the very rich. I just couldn't believe it.

While we were doing calisthenics at the beginning of the morning practice session, I noticed the second surprise. We were supposed to be running in place, but instead I sort of eased over to Pat Riley and said, "Gail's holding out, isn't he?"

"Yep," Pat said, grinning at me. "He wants them to renegotiate his contract. Cooke won't do it."

Gail Goodrich is in the last year of a three-year contract. A few of us talked about it after practice, and the consensus was that he's making about $150,000. A lot of money, but nowhere near what some of the other guards in the league are getting. In fact, somebody said there are 47 players in the NBA who make more money than Gail does. It's a cinch he knows that too and figures it isn't right for him to be that far down the list after making the All-Star team last year and leading the Lakers in scoring with 25.3 points a game. He is a ten-year veteran coming off the best year of his career and probably figures he is in the same league as the guards who are making from $200,000 to $400,000 a year: Walt Frazier, Nate Archibald, Jerry West, Earl Monroe, and so on.

It takes a lot of courage to hold out, though, because Gail knows he's risking his career in Los Angeles, which means a lot to him. He grew up here, was a star at UCLA, and is well known around town. And he knows the Lakers could trade him without a second thought for holding out. Last year, when Jerry West wanted to renegotiate his contract, it got to the point where they were going to sell him to Portland for $600,-000. And that was Jerry West, the last remaining superstar on the team and always the most popular with the fans. Eventually, he just showed up at an exhibition game in Reno. It's hard to believe that Gail could accomplish what Jerry couldn't. Cooke says he has a policy of never renegotiating a long-term contract (though there is talk he did for Wilt Chamberlain two years ago), and Gail's still has a year to go.

There are always a lot of rumors about trades at the beginning of any season, and Gail's holding out makes them even more prevalent now. You hear he might go to Phoenix for Charlie Scott or to Cleveland for Austin Carr. You hear that Zelmo Beaty, a veteran center for Utah of the ABA, has played out his option and we might get him. You hear Kermit Washington might go to Phoenix for nobody knows who.

While a few of us were talking about this at the end of the second practice session today, Bill Bridges climbed out of the whirlpool. "Just keep me off the waiver list," he said. The waiver list is the first step to being cut from the team. And when you're 35 years old and in your thirteenth year like Bill is, it's the first step out of the league.

SEPTEMBER 21

Before the morning practice today Bill Sharman said again that he really wants us to put out in these drills, that they are very important because they will determine who is going to play and who isn't. "Nobody has a position nailed down," he said, "and the statistics we're keeping in practice are going to be very important."

Bill is a nut on statistics, even from the first day of practice. He keeps figures on the shooting drills in the morning session and on the scrimmages in the evening session. When we're moving around the key taking our jump shots from various positions, somebody's there writing down how many we make and how many we miss. When we play a game of 21, with teams of three players going against each other, they're keeping stats. When we shoot free throws at the end of practice, they count those too. Then they break down the figures individually and post them, and that's supposed to determine the intrasquad lineups for the next day. The only problem is, they don't go by the numbers.

When the statistics were posted today, Cazzie Russell and I had the best shooting percentages among the forwards, but it didn't affect who played with whom. Cazzie and Happy Hairston, and sometimes Connie Hawkins, were still working with what is clearly the first team—Elmore Smith at center and Jerry West and Jim Price at guard—while Bill Bridges and I were with Pat Riley and three rookies: Jeff Victor, Seymour Reed, and Brian Winters. Occasionally, Bill Sharman will mix it up, but it's clear what his thinking is. He's not paying any attention to those statistics. Maybe he shouldn't—what difference does it make how you do in a game of 21? But then why make such a big deal out of it?

It's so hard to get a line on anything this early, anyway. Bill is an absolute fanatic about working as hard in practice as in a game, and of course those of us who want to make an impression on him try to. But the more secure ballplayers tend to just go through the motions, and that can be catching. For instance, to guard a guy like Connie Hawkins can be a drag because he just doesn't practice hard. He plays the games hard, but in practice both he and the guy guarding him can look bad because they both end up playing at his energy level. There is a double standard, I guess, and there's some justification for it. You don't need an all-out effort in practice to know what the Hawk can do. He's proved it in hundreds of games. But what I have to do is not let the tempo he or anybody else sets affect me. My pace has to be ahead of everyone else's. I have to be at an intensity level of ten where some of the other guys can cruise through at seven.

The best way to handle it is not to think about it, just go out and bust your ass no matter what the other guys are doing. Pat Riley is the best example on our team, and the coaches are always pointing him out as a model for the rest of us. Pat is a real pep leader, a let's-run-ten-more-windsprints-coach type of guy who seems not only to know his place, which is to come off the bench, but consistently comes into a game and performs well. Pat always says he doesn't care if they play him or not just as long as they keep him.

Actually, he does a hell of a job when you consider his handicap: he can't see. I mean, he is almost blind. I personally gave him his nickname: TV (for tunnel vision) Riley. It's hard to believe when you see him popping 25-foot jumpers, but he has great difficulty picking up guys even when they're standing wide open. In fact, there are some guys who almost refuse to play when he's in the game.

Once last season Elmore Smith came out of a game and said, "I ain't playing any more, man. That guy ain't worth shit."

Another time I was standing wide open inside the other

team's center and Pat didn't see me; he took a long shot instead. After the game some of the guys started kidding me: "Pat missed you pretty bad, didn't he?"

"Pat, I am going to have to get you some wide-angle contacts," I said.

Bill Sharman almost fell over laughing.

SEPTEMBER 23

We haven't even been working out a week yet and everybody seems tired, irritable, and bored. These twice-a-day practice sessions drive everybody up the wall. It's the routine that gets you down. It never changes and the monotony wears you out.

We come out onto the Loyola gym floor and shoot around for a while. Then we do calisthenics and stretching exercises. Then we run laps, 20 at a time, with Bill Sharman saying, "A little slower" or "A little faster." By the time we've done 15, some guys are starting to fade. Then we scrimmage until we're ready to drop. The only bright spot is that we open the exhibition season in two days—against the Warriors in Santa Barbara —and at least that will break up the routine. But when we don't play, it will be two practices a day until the season starts, which isn't until October 18 because the league schedule opens a week late this year. I think it's because they don't want to compete with the World Series any more than they absolutely have to. Of course, that means the final playoff round won't be over until June. JUNE!

Last year Bill wanted us to keep practicing twice a day even after the regular season began because we'd had such a bad record in the exhibition games. We had finished a morning workout at the Forum when Bill told us to be back at 5:30.

"Wait a minute," a couple of guys said, and we all just sat down on the floor.

"Bill, we don't think we should be practicing twice a day at this point," Jerry West said.

I couldn't believe it. I was new on the club and nothing like this had ever happened at Baltimore. In fact, ever since I'd been playing, I'd believed a coach could do whatever he wanted. If he wanted the team to practice twice a day in the middle of the season, that was up to him. So I was very quiet.

"Well, you guys stink," Bill said. "You're getting killed. I feel we should have two practices."

But one of the older guys said, "We've never practiced twice after a certain point."

And I'll be damned if we didn't pretty much get our way. We ended up with one long practice—extending 15 or 20 minutes beyond the usual time.

About now guys are starting to feel some physical effects of the first week of all-out workouts. Connie Hawkins has missed two days with an infected toe and Jerry West has been out several days with a throat infection. He says he inhales so fast when he's running that it hurts his throat.

Jerry came into practice the other day and bawled out Frank O'Neill in this high-pitched voice of his that makes him sound like a chirping bird: "God damn, Frank. You gave me some shit that almost killed me." Frank takes a lot of abuse from us at times. A trainer is really in a funny situation. He's an important part of the team—helping with injuries, taping your ankles, giving rubdowns—yet he takes a lot of crap nobody else has to put up with. Frank is our emotional scapegoat, I guess. But he takes it pretty good-naturedly, and we all think a lot of him.

In the few days Jerry has practiced he's really looked great. He seems to be completely over the groin injury that kept him out most of last season. It will be nice to see him play healthy for once. It is an education just to watch him. There are some guards—West, Oscar Robertson, maybe Walt Frazier —who add a whole new dimension to the game. Some players can see one move ahead, but Jerry seems to see three or even four moves ahead. He plays the game as intelligently as anybody I've ever seen. And do we need him! Last exhibition season, when Jerry was holding out and we were playing poorly, you could just see the whole team waiting for him to come back.

"Don't worry, guys," Happy Hairston said after one loss. "The name of the game is Gerald West. You just can't play Jimmy Price in his place." This did not exactly endear Happy to Jim, of course.

Then when Jerry was injured during the season and it became clear that he wasn't coming back, you could see the whole attitude of the team go down a few levels. We really depend on him—psychologically as well as physically, I think. Jerry knows it too, and he did everything he could to get well so he could play last year.

Once last season I was sitting in the middle of the trainer's room, lacing up my shoes or something, when Jerry walked in with Dr. Kerlan. He went over to one of the benches and lay down and pulled down his pants. Dr. Kerlan felt around for a minute and asked him where it was hurting. Then he pulled out a giant needle and emptied it into Jerry's groin. Novocaine, I guess, or cortisone. Jerry's face turned red and he started sweating. I could tell that the pain was just unreal. It was freaky to watch. And it didn't do Jerry any good.

Another guy who's hurting is Elmore Smith. They've already taken two big syringes full of fluid out of his knees. It seems awfully early for that. If I had to pick the one guy who's under the most pressure on the Lakers this year, it would have to be Elmore. His biggest problem is that he isn't Wilt Chamberlain. That gives him something in common with everybody else in the world, of course, but the Lakers don't seem to see it that way. Last season, when Wilt was in the process of leaving Los Angeles and signing with San Diego of the ABA, the Lakers sent Jim McMillian, one of the best young forwards in the league, to Buffalo for Elmore. Elmore is 7-1 and weighs 250, but it was only his third year in the league and nobody has ever dominated the game the way Wilt did. It was unrealistic of the Lakers to expect miracles. There were times, though, when Elmore looked like a second coming. He once blocked 17 shots in one game, a league record, and he scored well at times too. But he just never reached a consistently high level.

I am an Elmore Smith fan. He is one of the nicest people I have ever met, a big-hearted, friendly country guy from Macon, Georgia. In fact, I think the whole pro basketball scene might be a little too much for him. He's just never been into the game a lot. He didn't even play it until his senior year in high school.

When Elmore plays well, it makes it so much better for everyone on the team. If he could find a way to just bottle his best nights, go out and play his ass off regularly, we'd win a lot more games. A *lot* more games. But the Lakers have never been able to figure out how to keep him motivated, and with Elmore that's essential.

Bill Bridges asked him the other day how much longer he was going to play and Elmore said, "A couple more years."

"Man, with all the money you're making," Bill said, "I wish I could do that."

"Well, I didn't ask for it," Elmore said.

I know that's exactly how he feels too, because last year he told me about the time he signed his contract with Buffalo, which was one of the biggest deals in the league. The signing took place in the New York office of Walter Kennedy, the commissioner of the NBA. Elmore's college coach was there along with his agent and some of the Buffalo brass.

"We think you can be just as good as Bill Russell," Kennedy said. "Since you are getting all this money, we expect you to perform like that. Are you going to be able to do it?"

"I don't know, man," Elmore said. "Don't ask me. Ask him." And he pointed to his agent.

Elmore is also an extremely religious man—I have great respect for him because he's truly sincere about it—and that added to the pressure last year. He and his wife, Jessica, who is really a nice lady, are devout Jehovah's Witnesses, and people were always coming over to meet at his house. Elmore would come home from practice or after games or off road trips, and they'd be there for meetings when all he really wanted to do was rest. It was getting him down to the point where he was playing poorly for a while. But about a month and a half before the end of the season he put his foot down and told them he'd see them after the season was over. From then on he averaged almost 20 points a game and was a big reason why we made it into the playoffs. I've got my fingers crossed that he can pick up this year right where he left off.

SEPTEMBER 24

Score one for the rumor mill. We got Zelmo Beaty today.

It's kind of a complicated deal. Zelmo has been with the Utah Stars of the ABA for the last four years and his contract is up. He'll be 35 next month, has had some knee problems, and his scoring average has gone down in each of the last three years. So it looks as if Utah didn't want to give him another big contract.

The Warriors still had the NBA rights to Zelmo so actually the Lakers bought him from them. It all seems sort of strange because we haven't yet compensated the Warriors for Cazzie Russell, who played out his option with them and then signed on with us. There's supposed to be some decision by the commissioner about whether Cazzie will cost the Lakers anything and, if so, how much. But you'd think the Warriors would be angry at the Lakers and not let us have another player they have the rights to.

Nevertheless, Zelmo joins us tomorrow in Santa Barbara for the exhibition season opener. There's no question he will be strictly a backup player for Elmore because of his age and his knees, but he's supposed to be a smart player and a nice guy. Bill Sharman coached him at Utah for a year and is very enthusiastic about getting him.

Elmore is happy Zelmo is coming too. He knows he can use help and he thinks it will do him a lot of good to practice against a quality center. He feels the Lakers have done something constructive to help him out for a change instead of just getting on him all the time. I think so too.

SEPTEMBER 25

We opened the exhibition season against the Warriors tonight. The less said the better. We looked raggedy on offense, didn't get back well on defense, got killed on the boards, and lost the game. I played 12 minutes and scored six points.

Bill Sharman was mad and I don't blame him. Even though it's very early and we are without Gail Goodrich, Jerry West, and Connie Hawkins, we have to win every game we can. We must start working together as a team and build up some confidence. A game like tonight's makes you wonder if there is anything to be confident about. It was a long ride home from Santa Barbara.

SEPTEMBER 26

I walked into the trainer's room to get taped for practice, but I had to wait a minute because somebody was ahead of me. It was Gail Goodrich. He looked up and broke into a smile. I grinned at him and walked over and shook his hand. We made small talk for a minute and that was it. His holdout had ended. Nobody asked him about the negotiations and he didn't volunteer anything, but it's pretty clear what happened. His contract was not renegotiated. Jack Kent Cooke and Pete Newell issued a gracious little statement to the press about how happy they were that he'd joined the team and that was the end of it. Everybody was awfully glad to see Gail, of course. I don't know how we're going to do with him this year, but I have a pretty good idea what we'd do without him. We'd lose.

The rumor mill never quits: Bill Bridges' latest one is that they're trying to put together a big package to get rid of Connie Hawkins. Somebody else said maybe they'd send him to the Warriors to pay for Cazzie Russell. This is going to go on from now until the trading deadline in February. You just have to live with it.

SEPTEMBER 27

We played our first exhibition game at the Forum tonight and I got there early so I could collect my thoughts before the game. Outside the locker room I ran into Jerry West's teenage son, David, and I stopped to talk for a minute. I told him to be sure his dad takes him to the Elton John concert at the Forum next week and he said they already had tickets.

While I was getting taped, I sat next to Jerry so I could tell him what a nice kid I think David is.

"Yeah, I know," Jerry said. "You won't find my kids like a lot of these brats you see nowadays."

I smiled and looked away to see how the taping was going. I almost missed what Jerry said next. He lowered his voice and was almost mumbling at me.

"I told David this might be the last game I ever play," he said, "and you know what he said? He said he was glad, that if that's what I want, that's what he wants."

I felt like somebody had kicked me in the head.

"God damn it, Jerry!" I finally blurted out. "Don't do it *now*. Some of us have never played basketball with you and would really like to. Stay around one more year."

"Yeah, I'd like to," he said. "But I'm kind of tired." He got up and walked away. After the game—he scored 19 points and had two steals and three assists in 32 minutes—I saw him grab Bill Sharman and take him over into a corner.

He's really serious, I thought. He's really going to do it.

We lost the game to Portland 92–91. It was Bill Walton's first game with the Trail Blazers and I was impressed. You know he's going to score and get his rebounds, but the thing that surprised me was how well he moves, how quick he is. Of course, pro ball is much rougher than the game he was used to at UCLA, but if he does well Portland could give us trouble in our division this year.

I think I was in a very good spot to make a judgment on Walton, as a matter of fact. I saw the whole game from the bench. I didn't know whether to be embarrassed or hurt or angry, so I guess I was all three. Early in the game I was really thinking about it, watching the ball, observing the forwards, trying to stay loose and ready on the bench. I didn't think much of it when I didn't get in during the first period, but when the whole second quarter went by too, I began to realize what was up. I was still hopeful, though, and at halftime in the locker room I did jumping jacks, ran in place, and then went back out on the floor and shot around hard for a few minutes to get my blood circulating.

In the third period the anger really started to build up. I thought about my family and friends who were in the stands to see me play for the first time this season. It was only an exhibition game. The team wasn't established. The positions weren't set. We all needed work. It didn't make any sense. During timeouts I made sure to be in the spot I always go to —just in range of Bill's left eye—so he would be aware of my presence and know I was concentrating on what he was saying.

A few minutes into the fourth quarter I *knew* I wasn't going to play. I was thinking really hateful things about everybody around me. I was as mad as I can get and still have self-control. I hated Bill. For a moment, I swear it, I could have beat the living shit out of him. A few minutes after the game, of course, I'd calmed down. Not to the point where I could forget what had happened, but at least to where that blind hatred was gone.

Cheryl and I had promised some friends down the block to stop by a party after the game. Most of the people there had been at the Forum. They all had a comment about what had happened.

"Doesn't he like you?" one girl said.

"You'd think he would play you because you grew up here," somebody else said.

One guy even wondered if Bill was testing me, trying to see if I'd give him a hard time about it.

But after about 20 minutes the conversation turned to other things and everything was all right. I was still disappointed and mad and hurt, but I made up my mind to forget what happened and try to go on from here. By the time I had something to eat and something to drink, I felt a little better. We left the party early so I could catch a plane for Oakland in the morning.

SEPTEMBER 28

Before our game against Seattle in Oakland tonight—it was the first half of a doubleheader—we heard a lecture on narcotics from a researcher at Johns Hopkins University. It's part of an NBA campaign that has been going on for several years now. The league used to be quite concerned about drugs. In Baltimore we had some heavy team meetings where they told us narcotics agents had been hired to follow certain teams. That didn't surprise me particularly. A similar situation arose in the rock music business not too long ago. The Beach Boys and other famous groups were under surveillance and were followed around on the road too.

But lately I sense less apprehension among NBA officials over drugs. Maybe it's because public attitudes are changing. Or perhaps it's because of the few well-publicized pot arrests involving some stars. Those busts were eventually thrown out of court, with no ill effects on the players or their teams, and there was little or no fan reaction. So nowadays the NBA settles for public statements on its vigilance against drugs and team lectures like the one we heard tonight.

There's no use pretending that pro basketball players aren't familiar with street drugs and that a lot of them don't turn on. We all went to college, and I doubt if there is any campus today where the students aren't exposed at least to marijuana.

On the Lakers the subject of drugs is kept very quiet. Even when it pops up in casual conversation—which it is going to do any time you get 12 guys together who read the papers or watch television—nobody ever really says much. You'll see some smiles and a few guys looking around the room, but the conversation usually dies pretty quickly. There is a real reluctance to talk about it.

Another way ballplayers relieve tension and relax is by having a few drinks. The drinkers, at least the ones I know fairly well, tend more toward beer than hard liquor. It might be because beer is the one acceptable substance with any kick to it allowed in the locker room. After a game I have seen Mike Riordan sit down and polish off a six-pack before he even got into the shower. And while he was having dinner or a snack after the game, he could easily drink ten beers at a sitting. I remember asking him once how he could drink so much and he grinned and said, "Well, you lose a lot of water during a game and you have to replenish your system."

I don't think it ever really hurt Mike, though, because he's such a dedicated athlete. He has a tremendous amount of energy and works very hard at practice and in the games.

The guy from Johns Hopkins didn't talk about prescription drugs today. It occurs to me that for all the drug warnings and lectures I've heard over the years, very little attention has been paid to amphetamines and barbiturates the way it is in other sports. As far as I know, nobody in professional basketball uses them unless a doctor tells him to. It is possible that there might be some pill poppers in the NBA, but if there are they're keeping it very quiet. I've been on two teams and have some tight friends on a lot of the other ones, and I've asked around about it. The consensus is that nobody is taking the pills you read about in other sports.

I think the major reason is that we play so much. Say you start out with a game every other night and you take a pill to get up for them. Pretty soon you'll be playing every night and you'll be taking pills twice as often. It won't be long before you'll start developing a tolerance, and to get the right effect you'll have to take two a night and then three. By the time you get to the eighty-second game, you'll be fried. So I think basketball players just stay away from it to begin with. It's not the same thing as in football, where you would only need speed 20 times a year and would have a week between games to let the effects wear off.

There's another reason for the lack of pills in basketball, and I can attest to this one personally. My own experience with them was very brief while I was in college. It seemed as if everybody, not just athletes, was experimenting with something then, and I tried a Dexedrine pill a couple times to see what the effects would be. We generally played on Friday and Saturday nights and I never considered taking anything for the first game because with the week to get ready I had a lot of energy and didn't feel I needed any boost. But if I went to a party after the game and felt tired on Saturday, I could see why a guy might take a pill to get awake and ready to go. I would say there were three or four guys on the team who were doing this. I never had any trouble telling who they were. When I saw a 6–2 teammate standing underneath the basket during warmups suddenly jump up and dunk the ball, it wasn't hard to figure he must be on something.

Some of the effects of the pills I took seemed positive as far as my game was concerned. I could jump higher, run farther, regain my wind faster. And I found it was harder for guys to guard me when I was on something. You can easily tell when a player is wired because he runs around faster than normal—like a film that has been speeded up—and it is hard to keep up with him.

But the problem I found with Dexedrine was that the effects were unpredictable. I had some good games, but I also had some that weren't even close to average. There is such a thing as being too hyper, too wound up, and in a game like basketball, where touch is everything, that can ruin your game. If you're too wired, you can shoot over the basket or run right into guys and foul them without knowing what you're doing.

It's not the same as football, where a guy might want something that will make him slam into somebody harder. At a lot of positions brute strength is more important than touch or finesse. I've read that quite a few baseball players take pills, and that's a touch game, of course. Maybe they need something to keep awake.

The guy who spoke to us today was quite interesting. When he started talking about the effects that marijuana, cocaine, and heroin had on your body, I asked him if he'd ever tried them and was surprised when he said he had.

"Have you really tried heroin?" I asked.

"Yeah," he said. "Under lab conditions at Johns Hopkins."

"Well, how was it?" I asked. I've always wondered what it is about heroin that would make somebody want it so much he'd become addicted to it.

"It was a good feeling," he said. "One of the best I've ever had."

I was really interested now—both at finding an expert who would talk so openly and honestly and at hearing what he had to say—but I realized some of the guys were starting to snicker. Sort of "Look at Love trying to get the inside information. Isn't that funny?"

To me, it was just an educational experience. Here was a guy who actually knew what heroin was like, but I guess they figured it was just crazy Stan Love acting up again. Will I ever shake that image?

By the time the game against Seattle started, I began to get a better perspective on why I hadn't played last night. I think I may even see it from Bill Sharman's point of view, especially the pressure he's under. This is the fifteenth season the Lakers have been in Los Angeles, and they have always made the playoffs. It's simply expected by the fans, the press, and the front office that we'll be a contender every year, which makes it a very difficult situation. You're just not supposed to lose. And it all weighs very heavily on Bill.

Toward the end of last season the Warriors, who had been hot, were ahead of us in the division. The playoffs had been set up so the four teams in each of the two conferences with the best won-lost percentage got into them, and it was clear that only the winner in our division was going to make it. I remember once, after a loss to Golden State, Bill had met with reporters and seemed really disturbed because everybody had asked him what was wrong and how he felt about being perhaps the first Laker coach not to make the playoffs.

"God," he said, "you would think these people would give us a little credit for being where we are right now after losing both Wilt and Jim McMillian and with Jerry being hurt. We're still in it, but they don't give us credit for what we've accomplished to this point. It's depressing."

He was really bothered that we couldn't get recognition for what we'd done with a team that was far inferior to some of the Laker clubs of the past. We were counted out from the very beginning, yet we finally did get into the playoffs with a team that was thrown together almost at the last minute and had never really played as a unit.

The front office and the coaches feel this pressure from the public and the press, which is bad enough, but the players get it from all sides: public, press, owners, coaches, other players. I think this is especially true in Los Angeles because the fans have been spoiled by so many good teams. The shit that will come down the year the Lakers don't make the playoffs will be unbelievable, I think.

The best example of this demanding attitude on the part of the Los Angeles fans was the way they responded to Wilt Chamberlain. All he did, of course, was dominate nearly every game he played for the Lakers with rebounds and defense. Wilt was a superspecialist by that point in his career, and sometimes you could watch him almost taking pride in refusing to shoot. It was as if he wanted to prove he could be great

40

without ever scoring a point and that the Lakers could win that way too. And they did. He took them down to the finals of the playoffs several times. But it wasn't enough. He got an incredible amount of abuse from the fans, the press, and finally from the team itself, I think. So he just walked away from it.

It seemed amazing to me at the time. Wilt is perhaps the greatest basketball player in the history of the game, a man absolutely secure in his job and talent. He was getting paid $400,000 a year, had built a beautiful home, and had established exactly the kind of life he wanted for himself: volleyball on the beach, television commercials, movie stars for friends, women coming out of his ears. But he chucked it all so he could commute by plane to San Diego every day—to a job as player-coach where he wasn't even allowed to play because of legal hassles and to a team that competed in an inferior league and in a small gym before tiny crowds. Sure, he got more money, but how much more could he use? Finally, I think, even with Wilt the pressure got to be too much and he had to get away from it. This is what he told *Sports Illustrated* when he retired from basketball this year:

"It had gotten to the point with the Lakers that the only thing you were appreciated for was if you won it all. If you didn't do that, you hadn't done your job."

I don't think it's changed a bit.

I've saved the best for last. We beat the hell out of Seattle 127–99, and Bill remembered that I was on the team. I played 18 minutes and scored ten points. But that isn't the half of it.

Four reserves—Bill Bridges, Kermit Washington, Brian Winters, and I—went into the game in the second quarter when we were down by about 12 points. By halftime we were up by six, and Bill left us in for the whole third quarter. By the time we came out, we were ahead by 13. I felt about 1,000 percent better than last night. My sister and her husband were in the stands—it was easy to pick them out because she'd just broken her leg water-skiing—and when I looked up at them they were laughing and enjoying themselves.

All the guys on the bench were happy too. Bill told us that

41

if we won the game we wouldn't have to practice tomorrow. But when you look up at the scoreboard in the second quarter and see that you are down by a dozen points you start figuring what's the latest you can get up the next day and still be at the gym on time. After ten straight days of double sessions, everybody was cheering us on when we started to turn it around.

I was really ready when Bill sent me in. The first thing I did was crash into a Seattle player under the boards and commit a foul. But after that I settled down. We were all playing good defense—the Sonics got only 19 points in the second quarter and 18 in the third—and my shooting touch was there when I wanted it. If I can just get to the point where I know I'll play a certain number of minutes a game, I'll really be happy. It's not important to start, only to know that you're in the rotation and will get a certain amount of time. That way, you can go all out and stay in beautiful shape.

Since we played the first game of the doubleheader, we were able to catch a plane that got us home before midnight. Cheryl met me at the airport and she, Brian Winters, and I went out to a bar in the Marina. On the way, she said Chick Hearn had really sounded excited on the radio about the play of the reserves. At one point he said something about "Stan Love, who did such a *great* job . . ." Can it be true? Is Chick starting to come around?

We were in a very good mood at the bar. One singer did such a good imitation of Ray Charles that we thought he might be lip-syncing to a tape. And we enjoyed talking to Brian too, who looks like he's really going to help the team. He scored 20 points tonight and has great poise for a rookie. Brian is from Rockaway, N.Y.—completely over on the other side of the country—but he lives on the beach too. We shook hands over the fact that he has a 96 in his basement with a banana skag and teak rails. It's exactly the same surfboard that a lot of the guys I grew up with have in their basements.

POSTSCRIPT: Jerry West didn't make the trip. The Lakers said he had the flu.

SEPTEMBER 30

Bill Bridges and Jim Price were going after a loose ball in practice today when they collided. They pushed into each other hard for a second and had a few angry words before they finally calmed down. That sort of thing is starting to happen more and more often now. As it gets closer to the start of the season, the tension begins to build, especially among the rookies and the guys who might be expendable. They are trying so hard to do well that it can get intensely competitive. The trade rumors don't make the situation any easier, especially since it's clear that the Lakers are a long way from having an established team. It's like there's a big ax chasing you and you have to do everything you can to stay out of its path.

We were splitting up for a scrimmage—the gold team heading in one direction and our little band of reserves, the blue team, going the other way—when I shouted out, "OK, let's go, scrubeenies. Everybody down to the other end."

"I resent you calling me a scrubeenie," Pat Riley said.

"Well, what are you?" I asked him.

"I am a *professional* scrubeenie."

Didn't I say Pat had a good attitude?

The forward situation seems to have resolved itself pretty much the way I thought it would: Happy Hairston, Connie Hawkins, and Cazzie Russell in the playing rotation with Bill Bridges and myself in reserve. Brian Winters has looked so good that it's possible they won't try to obtain another guard and will go with five forwards this season. It's hard to tell. I do have a feeling, though, that I'll be staying here.

Things can always happen to change the situation, of

course, and they aren't always trades. While we were working on defense today, Bill Sharman showed me a few things he wanted me to work on and told me I should stay ready in case of injuries. I said I would, but it seems like a drag for somebody to have to get hurt for me to get some playing time. So I am becoming aware that this might be another season like my first three. I am not going to be traded to a place where I can play, and I am not going to move Connie or Happy or Cazzie out of their ten-year-veteran, experienced-forward roles.

The funny thing is, though, I am no longer as pissed off about it as I once was. I find myself looking at it this way: The Hawk is a hell of a ballplayer when he puts his mind to it. Happy was the best rebounding forward in the league last year. And Cazzie is a scoring machine. To play behind them, to push them in practice so they'll play better, and to know I could play as well as any of them if given the chance puts me in a better mood.

OCTOBER 3

We had a morning shootaround to get ready for the intrasquad game tonight and it ended just as the Lakers were starting a press conference to announce officially that Jerry West was retiring. I told Elmore Smith that it was a pretty heavy moment in basketball history and we should be there. So we went upstairs to the Forum press room and stood near the wall behind the television cameras and reporters.

It's been six days since Jerry told me he was retiring and they can't have been the most pleasant ones of his life. During practice at Loyola yesterday Jerry walked in, looking a little shaken. We all knew where he'd come from and nobody envied him. He'd been in a meeting with Jack Kent Cooke and there had been only one subject on the agenda: trying to get Jerry to change his mind. Cooke is an extremely strong-willed person and he's used to getting his way. Also, Jerry has talked about quitting before and then not gone through with it, so Cooke might have thought he could get him to change his mind again.

But when I asked Jerry if he was really through, he said, "Yeah. I'm glad I don't have to be out there with you right now."

I'll bet he was glad he didn't have to be in Cooke's office any more too.

I think it came to Jerry all of a sudden that he isn't 27 years old any more and that he can't do now all the things he could then. The fact that he is still superior to almost every other guard around doesn't matter to him. He has his own standards, and once he can't reach them any more that's it. Also, I think he's finally had enough basketball.

I don't think any of the other players doubt he's serious this time either. We've already started talking about him in the past tense. When we were getting taped for practice yesterday, Bill Bridges started getting on Gail a little, saying, "All this means, Goodrich, is that all the guards in the league are going to double-team you and it's going to make it that much harder on you."

Gail didn't say anything, but I'm sure a lot of thoughts are going through his mind about Jerry's quitting. For one thing, even though Bridges was kidding, what he said was absolutely true. When Jerry was out hurt most of last season, Gail actually had his best year as far as scoring was concerned because he had to take up the shooting slack in the backcourt. But Gail knew the team suffered, and I really think he loves playing with Jerry. Also, Gail must be kicking himself for not holding out one more week. It wasn't the best timing in the world to come back only a few days before Jerry retired. If he'd waited until afterward, negotiations might have swung around in his favor. No team can afford to lose a Jerry West *and* a Gail Goodrich.

The one person I think will be affected the most by Jerry's retirement is Jim Price. He's only in his third year, but he averaged 15.4 points a game last season and the Lakers are hoping he'll develop into a high-scoring guard as well as a playmaker like Jerry. But I think Jim needs time to become a quarterback-type guard. He's awfully young and inexperienced to be running the team. A guy like Jerry, or like Archie Clark when he was with Baltimore, is constantly creating things, making them happen not just for himself but for the team as a whole. It's a gift to be able to do this, and for all his skill Jim just isn't able to yet. In a way, Jim is in a good situation now because he'll get his chance in a hurry. But there will be a lot of pressure on him too. If we don't win, he'll get a lot of the blame. I know *I* would not want to be the guy who had to replace Jerry West.

At the press conference I saw that even though the players seem to have accepted Jerry's retirement, the front office is having a hard time getting used to it. First, Pete Newell spoke about what a loss he will be to the team; then Bill Sharman said it was a shame he was retiring at this time because he is in perfect shape and could be All-League again this season. But then Jerry spoke and things got a little lighter. He's always gotten along well with the press, and when the reporters started asking questions you could feel the rapport he's developed with them over the years.

It surprised me that Elmore and I were the only players there. I wondered if maybe we shouldn't have come, but later tonight, after the intrasquad game, Jerry came into the locker room and thanked me. "A lot of people might not think that I would care about something like that or have feelings about it," he said. "But it meant a lot to me to see that you were there."

I was touched and thought how in character it was for him to think about that when so many other things must have been going through his mind. We're going to miss Jerry a hell of a lot on the court this year. I'm going to miss him off it too.

A couple of thousand people crowded into the Loyola gym for the intrasquad game tonight. It's a game the Lakers play every year for a scholarship fund at the university, and being in that little gym, packed to the rafters, made me feel I was back in high school or college. A lot of my friends and family were there, and I put on a little show for them, scoring 27 points to lead the forwards on both teams. It was strictly gold against blue, like in a practice scrimmage, so we lost, but it was a good game and we all enjoyed playing it.

Afterward, a lot of people came into the locker room, including my brother Mike. He was wearing purple velvet pants, straw hat, Hawaiian puka shell necklace, and beads—just your typical low profile rock star outfit. I introduced him to Connie Hawkins and a few of the other guys and then Mike said, "Where is the coach? Let's go see the coach."

"Uh, Mike," I said, "we don't want to meet the coach tonight." I wasn't sure how Bill would take the puka shells and the velvet pants.

"No, no, come on," he said. "Where is he?"

"I tell you what," I said, pointing across the room. "He's over there. You go introduce yourself." I ducked into the shower.

A minute later the Hawk came in and grinned at me. "Your brother just freaked out the coach," he said.

"What do you mean?"

"I don't know, man," said Connie. "All he did was go over and say, 'I am Mike Love, Stan's brother,' but I think he just freaked him out because when your brother walked away Sharman just kept staring at him."

When I came out of the shower, Mike was gone and Kermit Washington was laughing at me. "I don't think Sharman was ready for your brother," he said.

"God, he's as freaky as you are," somebody else said. "I can see why you are the way you are."

Thanks, Mike. There goes all the hard work on the image.

OCTOBER 5

"WHAT NIGHT IS IT?!"
 "SATURDAY!"
 "WHAT?!"
 "IT'S SATURDAY!"

Elton John broke into "Saturday Night's Alright for Fighting" and 20,000 people at the Forum went wild. I mean *wild*. They stood on their feet, they sang, they danced, they stomped, they swayed. They just ate it up. Tonight is the second night I've seen him, and I'm going again tomorrow. That's three out of the four shows he's giving here, and I'm only sorry I had to miss one.

It's really a trip to sit in the stands at the arena you play in and be part of the audience. Instead of people watching you, you're digging on somebody else, relating to the performers and the crowd at the same time. And with all due respect to the caliber of the audience the Lakers draw, Elton John really brought them out. Steve McQueen was behind us tonight; Elizabeth Taylor made one of the shows and so did Ringo Starr. Not to mention nearly all the Lakers. Gail Goodrich, who is usually so quiet about everything, went to last night's show and was just raving about it at practice today. He couldn't stop talking. Pat Riley was singing Elton John songs all during practice. Jerry West took his whole family. I've been to a lot of rock shows, but Elton John is the best entertainer I've ever seen. Except for the Beach Boys, of course.

Tonight's concert marked the end of a very long day and I just sat back and dug the red carpet on the stage, Elton John's wild costumes, which would make Liberace look straight, and

48

the groovy music. I had to let the other 19,999 do most of the screaming, though. I was too beat. I got up early after last night's concert to go to practice and was really looking forward to a nap before the afternoon workout. But the Lakers' publicity director, Dick White, asked me if I'd fill in for Elmore Smith, who was supposed to make a couple of personal appearances in two department stores for a tennis shoe manufacturer. Elmore's ankles were really hurting him and he had to go to the doctor.

"Dick," I said, "I am really tired, I have practice again at five and I've got a concert to go to tonight."

"They'll pay you $250," he said.

"I'd love to."

So I drove home to change clothes, got to the downtown store about half an hour late, and found a bunch of kids and thousands of pictures of Elmore hanging all over the place. I had to go in and say, "Sorry, kids, I'm not Elmore."

After that I drove out to the Pasadena store, then to practice, then home, then to the concert. I hope Elton John didn't take it personally that I just applauded him from my seat instead of joining in the standing ovation.

OCTOBER 7

The reactions to Jerry West's retirement have been coming in. Harry Glickman, the general manager of the Trail Blazers, said he couldn't understand it judging from Jerry's performance against them in the one game he played.

"He took Geoff Petrie to the cleaners," Glickman said. "Petrie was so flustered he had to be taken out of the game."

Somebody mentioned that to Jerry and he said, "You just

don't remember the way I used to play."

Bill Bridges was asked what he thought. "I have nothing but envy for the man," he said.

Connie Hawkins hasn't found an apartment yet—I think he's waiting to see whether or not he's going to be traded—and he's living at a hotel near the airport. Over the weekend somebody set off a bomb in one of the hotel bathrooms. The cops think it might have been a member of the Symbionese Liberation Army, but they haven't caught anyone yet.

When I saw Connie at practice today, I played it very straight.

"Damn," I said, "I told those guys not to put it in the bathroom."

He cracked up. "It was close, Love, but not close enough."

I keep telling myself I have to have a completely different attitude toward guys like the Hawk this season. But it is difficult to work up an antagonism toward the guy who is maybe my closest friend on the team. How can you be competitive against somebody who is coming over to your house for dinner that night? How can you be enemies on the court when you're friends off the court? It would be a lot better if my friends on the Lakers were guards.

To be truthful, though, I don't have this problem with *every* forward on the team. It is hard for me to think about Happy Hairston without having tremendously mixed feelings. I have great respect for him as a basketball player—he is an unbelievable rebounder—and for his ability to communicate with the Laker staff. He hangs around the front office a lot and is always having long discussions with Pete Newell and Jack Kent Cooke. This helps him a lot in the long run, I think, and I wish I were better at it myself.

But we have just never been very close and I'm not entirely sure why. I guess part of it is that Happy does things that seem so strange to me. I suppose I must seem the same way to him, but anybody who will walk into a bar in the Marina wearing his Laker sweat suit with his name on the back and carrying his equipment bag with him is just too far out for me.

Or he'll hang around the Forum Club after games wearing a denim outfit with steel studs down the pants legs and on the back of his shirt forming the initials HHH, for Harold (Happy) Hairston. He seems to be digging on himself all the time, inviting people to turn on to him.

Happy does take some kidding about the way he comes on. Some of the older players call him Weird Harold, right to his face. Connie Hawkins, in fact, just uses the first part of it. He'll yell across the locker room, "Hey, Weird!" I don't think Happy's too fond of this, but that's the way it is. He has to live with his image the way I have to live with mine.

OCTOBER 8

Connie Hawkins got hit with another bomb today, one that struck even closer to home. It's all over town that the Lakers have put out the word to every team in the league that he's available. The interesting thing is that there haven't been any takers. It's like putting Hank Aaron on the waiver list and coming up empty.

I'm not sure there ever was a player with greater natural ability than the Hawk. There is nobody who could play one on one better than he could. He could shoot, he could drive to the basket, and he could make some of the most amazing passes you ever saw. He can still do some of these things, but Connie is 32 now and has played so many games in inferior leagues with inferior players that it's hard for him to be consistent. Also, I don't think he really has the desire he once did. How can you blame him after he was blackballed from the league during his prime years because of a phony gambling charge that was hung on him in college? The Hawk has paid his dues, and I don't think he has to answer to anybody about anything.

Connie is a great crowd favorite wherever he goes. In New York, where he was a sensational schoolyard player, he's almost a legend. When we were there for a game with the Knicks last year, I reminded him as we were finishing practice at the Garden that he'd been promising me a copy of the book David Wolf wrote about him, *Foul,* for a couple of months.

"OK," he said. "Let's go get it now."

So we walked a couple of blocks to a bookstore. As soon as we got out on the street, a crowd started gathering. "Hey, Connie Hawkins," people were saying. "How you doing, man? What's happening?" Connie started signing autographs and giving soul-brother handshakes and leading everybody toward the bookstore like the Pied Piper. When we went into the store, he didn't have to tell the salesman who he was. He just said, "Hey, can you find my book for me?" to one of the clerks. After he bought it, he went on signing autographs and shaking hands all the way back to the hotel. We were almost crushed by the time we reached the lobby because the crowd just kept growing and growing. Finally, Connie just told everybody, "Check me out at the Garden," and we escaped inside. I'd never seen anything like it.

But the Hawk has been through too much to be affected by any of it. When he found out today the Lakers were trying to peddle him, all he said was, "Well, they will do that to you." It was a lot different from my reaction when the same thing happened to me last year.

It's easy to find out when the front office is making a wholesale effort to trade you rather than just discussing some specific deal with one other club. They put the news out on a Telex wire that connects all the NBA teams. Of course, it quickly leaks out through one club or another, and sometimes the club initiating the move will leak the word to the press to get the ball rolling. I was really bugged when I found out the Lakers had made me available last season. I hadn't played much in the first few exhibition games; and then, just when I was starting to get in a little, I fell guarding Rick Barry in a game against the Warriors and cracked my kneecap. That put me out for three weeks and the Lakers made a quick deal with

Phoenix to get the Hawk. Later on, just when I was starting to get well, I heard they were trying to get rid of me. Here they had Connie, the lineup was established, and they were openly looking to trade me. It took the enthusiasm right out of me because I knew I wasn't in their plans. It just broke my spirit for a while.

In Connie's case, the Lakers might be trying to motivate him by putting the word out that he's available. Maybe they figure that even if they don't trade him, just the fact they have tried will light a fire under him. But I don't know if that will work with the Hawk. He's very much his own man and it's hard to get him to do something he doesn't want to do.

We drove to Bakersfield late in the afternoon for an exhibition game with Phoenix, and when I didn't play through most of the first three quarters I figured I wasn't getting in. But then I heard assistant coach John Barnhill call my name. Jesus, I thought, end of the third quarter. Why now? Very seldom does Bill Sharman put somebody in at that point if he hasn't played earlier.

We were down a few points, but with a team of scrubeenies—Kermit Washington, Brian Winters, Bill Bridges, Pat Riley, and myself—we managed to get things moving and put the game into overtime. We ended up winning 116–113 and were all feeling pretty good. I hope that by contributing like this I can convince Bill that I can be intense and quick coming off the bench and it will get me more playing time. I just wish I could figure out what his substitution pattern is so I can be ready for it.

Late tonight Bud Furillo, who is very knowledgeable and talks to the right people, discussed the Lakers' forward situation at some length on his radio show. He said Seymour Reed, the rookie, was looking good and that I'd done a few things coming off the bench. What it boiled down to, he said, was that the guy in trouble was Connie. Furillo mentioned that word about the Hawk had been put out to all the other clubs and strongly suggested that once the season began Connie would be gone.

OCTOBER 10

We played Seattle in Portland tonight—another exhibition doubleheader—and the Sonics were really out for blood. They got it too: mine and Cazzie Russell's.

The Sonics came out very aggressively, giving us a hard time from the start. Maybe it's because they haven't been doing very well so far, but whatever the reason their coach, Bill Russell, really had them clawing and scratching.

We were starting to fade a little in the second quarter when Bill Sharman put me in. I lasted all of 30 seconds. I ran up the court once and Seattle took a shot. As I turned to screen out my man—Leonard Gray, I think—his arm jammed in between the index and middle fingers of my right hand. It hurt some, but I didn't think much of it until I'd run down to the other end of the floor. Then I felt a twinge of pain and I looked down at my hand. There wasn't much blood, but it's a little disconcerting to see a hole in your hand. I walked over to the bench and Frank O'Neill put some ointment on it. Then he walked me into the trainer's room, where a doctor took three stitches in the fleshy area at the base of the fingers. He wrapped my hand in tape and said I'd be a spectator for a couple of days.

By the time I came back to the bench, the third quarter had started. We were down by a couple of points when Cazzie stole the ball and drove the length of the court. It was a complete breakaway and there was nobody in front of him so he went in for a casual layup. Suddenly, Slick Watts, a second-year guard, rushed up from behind and pushed Cazzie hard.

54

He tried to make the basket and his feet hit the ground while he was off balance. He fell on his butt, slid across the floor, and slammed into the upright holding the basket. Cazzie lay there, writhing in pain, while we all ran over to him. I was at the end of the bench so I got there first, thinking, God, how could Slick push him like that? It was a terrible thing to do. Cazzie had been way ahead of him and Slick really had to exert himself just to catch up. It was just a preseason game. How could you risk a guy's career like that? I could hear Chick Hearn calling it the most flagrant foul he had ever seen. It might have been.

We stood there for a minute and then Cazzie got up and ran up and down the court once or twice. He waited a minute to see if he felt any better, but it was clear he couldn't run. He went into the locker room.

We lost the game by two points, and afterward I sat near Cazzie drinking some juice and eating some almonds before taking my shower. He was soaking his leg in ice and taking it pretty well—though he did call Slick Watts some pretty unpleasant things. The mood in the locker room was surprisingly light considering the situation.

Connie Hawkins came over with a towel and some hot liniment—absolutely the worst thing for a leg injury—and said, "Here, let me help you out, Cazzie." And he jokingly tried to put some of the liniment on his leg.

Then Bill Bridges got into it, saying, "Yeah, Cazzie, let me help you." And he stumbled and acted like he was going to bump into him and rip up his leg even more. I looked across at Brian Winters and the look on his face said, "Oh, my God. Here's this guy with a bad leg injury and these guys are doing stuff like this."

Finally, Cazzie hobbled out on crutches to catch a plane for Los Angeles. Dr. Kerlan will examine him tomorrow while we are in Seattle and determine how badly he's hurt.

I took a shower with a plastic bag over my hand, holding my arm up in the air so it wouldn't get wet, and I tried to sort the whole thing out in my mind. I guess I'm going to get more playing time when my hand heals.

OCTOBER 11

We had a morning shootaround before our game with the Warriors in Seattle tonight, and afterward Bill Sharman called a meeting to discuss what was wrong with us. A lot of guys talked and said the usual things: we should dribble less, we should pass more, we should play team defense. The meeting was just breaking up when Frank O'Neill walked in.

"They're operating on Cazzie at four o'clock," he said. "His knee ligaments are all ripped up. He'll be in a cast for six weeks."

Everybody looked around the room and a couple of guys said, almost in unison, "Oh, shit." You could almost hear people thinking: six weeks in a cast, followed by a long recuperation period, followed by getting back in shape again. Cazzie would be gone for a long time, maybe the whole season. Slick Watts was not the Lakers' favorite fellow right about then.

The forwards started looking around at each other and it was fairly obvious what we were doing: counting heads. Jerry West was gone. Cazzie was gone. We were just about down to the 12-man limit. Barring trades, it looked like we all had the team made. Nobody was happy that Cazzie was hurt, but it was still kind of a relief. You get ambivalent feelings in situations like that. No matter how dedicated you are to the team and to winning games, everyone still thinks about his own situation.

Before the game there was another surprise. Pat Riley told me that, for a while at least, his days as a swing man rotating between forward and guard were over. "Bill told me he's starting me at forward tonight," Pat said. "I asked him if

56

he didn't want to start Connie now that Cazzie's out and said that maybe I could be helpful coming in off the bench. But he said no, he wanted to do it this way."

I could see what was going through Pat's mind. He'd never been anything but a reserve and usually at guard except when the other team had a short forward in the game, a guy like Bill Bradley or Mike Riordan. Pat's only 6-4 so he has trouble guarding the game's big forwards as well as rebounding. But Pat can shoot, and it's clear Bill has to try every possible combination. I wished him luck, but I'm not sure he heard me. Pat had a lot of thoughts running through his head.

I thought Pat did a fairly decent job against the Warriors, and considering the shape we're in, so did the team. Rick Barry sent the game into overtime with a jump shot at the buzzer, but we ended up winning. It was the first good news we'd had as a team in what seemed an awfully long time.

OCTOBER 13

We flew from Seattle to Phoenix yesterday for our game with the Suns tonight and I considered getting off in Los Angeles since there wasn't much I could do because of my hand. But Bill Sharman said I should stay in case he wanted to change any of the plays. So I ran through the practice session feeling like kind of a dummy because I couldn't handle the ball.

After this morning's shootaround I called Cheryl just to say hi. I hadn't talked to her in three days. She was cleaning the house and Steve was out on the beach, so we chatted a while and I went back to my room to order some room service, take a nap, and maybe watch the World Series. Then the phone rang. It was Cheryl again.

"Is it true you got traded?" she said.

"What do you mean is it true I got traded?" I said, wondering what the hell she was talking about.

"Well, a reporter just called and said he heard that you and Connie Hawkins and Pat Riley are going to Chicago for Bob Love."

"I haven't heard anything about it," I said. "Find Steve and tell him to call Pete Newell and find out what's happening."

All I could think was, There goes my nap. My whole day was ruined. My whole *day*. Hell, how about my whole *life?* I called Pat in his room and told him the news.

"Oh, my God," he said. "Not really."

Then I went down the hall and told Connie.

"Oh, my God," he said. "Chicago."

We could hear the baseball game as we stood in the hall pouting and feeling sorry for ourselves. We talked about the Bulls—who their forwards were and whether it was a good opportunity or not. Finally, I just sat down in the hall and said, "Shit," thinking of how cold it was in Chicago in the winter.

"I know what you mean," said the Hawk, and we sat there grumbling to each other.

I tried to call Bill Sharman, but he was at a women's tennis tournament so I couldn't find out anything right away. Finally, after what seemed like forever, Steve called and said he'd talked to Pete Newell, who'd denied the whole thing. Pete said he hadn't talked to Dick Motta, the Bulls' coach, or anybody else from the Chicago organization and that it just wasn't true.

"As of Sunday, October 13," Steve said, making a joke of it, "you are still a member of the Los Angeles Lakers." Very funny.

Pretty soon, I began getting calls from friends wanting to know why I wasn't in Chicago or at least on the way. I tried to find out from them how the rumor had started and finally was able to piece it together. Apparently, it had begun with some Chicago writers who were in Los Angeles for the World Series. Bob Love, who is a big, rugged forward (and no relation, by the way; we're as different as black and white), is holding out and trying to get the Bulls to renegotiate his contract. That gives credence to the notion that they might be trying to get rid of him, and apparently his agent is involved in spreading the rumor. It got on the wires and some guy on a Los Angeles radio talk show was reporting it as fact. Somebody said he'd tuned in on the middle of a call and one listener had said, "Yeah, we are going to miss Hawkins." Statements like that can develop a life of their own without any relation to the facts.

About 20 minutes before the game we finally saw Bill at the Phoenix arena. "I just heard about it," he said. "Listen, it isn't true. Don't worry about it."

I could see he was upset because a rumor like this five days before the season starts can upset a lot of people, which he sure doesn't need when he's trying to get things together and straighten out our problems. Pat and Connie and I had calmed down a little by then, but it's hard to wipe it out of your mind. I had a cold and a headache and my hand hurt and I had to just sit and watch us get beaten by the Suns.

During the flight back home after the game the Hawk suddenly got up and handed me something. What's this shit? I thought, and I looked down at a Continental Airlines schedule. Six nonstops daily to Chicago. I looked over at the Hawk and we both cracked up.

OCTOBER 16

As I was standing in the shower after practice at the Loyola gym today, still holding my right hand high in the air with that damn plastic bag on it, I saw Bill Sharman take Seymour Reed aside in the locker room and talk to him for a long time. I wondered what was going on—please, not another trade rumor—when John Barnhill came in to take his shower.

"What's Sharman talking to Seymour about?" I asked.

John was mimicking me, holding his hand above his head, and he said, "What they're talking about is this," and he brought his arm down hard, the flat of his hand perpendicular to the floor, like a guillotine.

"Yeah?!" I said.

"Yeah," he said.

Now *that's* a surprise. We're certainly not overloaded with forwards any more, and I thought Seymour had a chance to make the team even before Cazzie Russell got hurt. He played steady basketball for a rookie, shot really well, rebounded OK, and wasn't bad on defense. But when I thought about it some more, I could see what had happened. It just proves again that the Lakers are not the kind of team that will work a guy into the lineup slowly and let him develop. The one word they hate to use is "rebuilding."

Since they must win every year, they feel they need the kind of ballplayer who can help them right away. Either your skills are at the level to help the club win now or you're gone or on the bench. My own feeling is that you have to build a team, get good young players and work with them, put them into games at certain times and give them learning experience. This is what Boston, for example, has done with Paul Westphal. They let him play gradually for a couple of years and late last season he really came on and helped them.

But the Lakers don't like to take chances. They'd rather trade for the established guy they think can help them right away. They don't feel they can afford to be patient and develop their own players. Which is part of my problem, of course. I would love to be able to burst forth as a superplayer, but I think I'd stand a better chance of helping the team in the long run if I were just able to play a regular amount of time and gain experience instead of not knowing when or how much I'll play from game to game.

Later, Bill Bridges and Connie Hawkins and I talked

about how they cut Seymour right in front of everybody. It didn't seem to be a very professional way to handle it. The least they could have done was take him aside in private to give him the bad news.

OCTOBER 17

Bill Sharman's announcement of the starting lineup for our season opener with the Warriors tomorrow was in today's papers. The reporters seemed surprised that Pat Riley will open at forward with Happy Hairston. None of us is surprised, though. Pat has been working with the first team in practice since he started that exhibition game in Seattle last week. But I guess the press just naturally assumed that with Cazzie out, Connie Hawkins would be the starter. It would contradict everything Bill preaches, however, for him to start the Hawk now. Pat has really been working hard in practice and Connie has been himself. He just can't get psyched up for practice.

I can see that in the past this might not have been as important. In the years when the Lakers had players like Wilt Chamberlain, Jerry West, and Elgin Baylor they could come to practice, run up and down a few times without really busting their asses, and still go out and win by 20 points. It may be that when Jerry retired—cutting the final link with the past— Bill realized he had a team without great stars and he would have to demand the same effort from everyone. I also think Bill is still trying to motivate the Hawk and figures that if he leaves him on the bench, he'll work to get off it. We'll see.

Mal Florence of the Los Angeles *Times* had an interesting piece today under the headline "Where Have All the Superstars Gone?" Because of retirements, injuries, and contract disputes, the NBA season is opening without the following players: Jerry West, Oscar Robertson, Wilt Chamberlain, Kareem Abdul-Jabbar, Dave Cowens, Cazzie Russell, Willis Reed, Dave DeBusschere, Jerry Lucas, Bob Love, Norm Van Lier, and Jeff Mullins. In truth, I think there are fewer *great* players around these days but more good ones. This makes for better competition, a more balanced league, and it also makes good coaching more important. Without the superstars, the line separating the players' abilities is a lot thinner; there are more intangibles for the coaches to judge.

Anyway, during practice Bill Bridges started needling Gail about the article.

"Hey, Goodrich, did you read the paper today?" he shouted at him. "There are no legitimate superstars on this team. Goodrich, did you hear that? Now give up the ball!"

Gail kept his usual poker face, but everybody else laughed pretty hard.

OCTOBER 18

A lot of players in the NBA like to pretend they're just doing a job, like laying bricks or raking leaves, and that they don't get excited or emotionally involved. I've never believed it. All we're really doing is playing a game, one you see kids playing in every schoolyard in America. In a way, we're just a bunch of kids too. Even with all the money and all the pressure and all the hassle, we're still little boys in a sense. Little boys who haven't totally grown up.

You can feel the excitement in the locker room before a game, especially the first one of the season, which is the goal you've been heading for during all those twice-a-day practice sessions. Pretty soon, when the games start following one another so fast that the end of the last one seems to bump into the beginning of the next, things can get pretty tedious. But it's easy and natural to get up for the season opener.

Before the game with the Warriors tonight, guys were hurrying to get dressed and loosening up and taping their feet and putting liniment on their legs. Bill Sharman was going over his plans, how to handle the Warriors offensively and defensively. Frank O'Neill was helping with the tape and giving rubdowns. A couple of guys were out on the court shooting a few baskets and some others were just sitting quietly, thinking.

Everybody has his own little mannerisms and rituals before a game. Some players like to talk, almost constantly, it seems. Bill Bridges was chattering about where the team is headed, who's going to be traded, what the latest rumor is. Sometimes he will talk about the strangest things. Once I heard him say, apropos of absolutely nothing, "How many of you guys are into guys?" Just like it was the most normal subject in the world to talk about before a game. It was strange. Here we were trying to get our minds unscrambled before a game and Bill was talking about something as bizarre as that. After a while, I think, his chatter gets on some guys' nerves, but Bill is so jovial about it—there's never anything mean or derogatory in what he says—that he loosens us up and is probably a good influence.

Other guys just sit and try to get themselves together. Elmore Smith, for instance, almost never has anything to say before a game. Jerry West was like that, always thinking intently about the game and the player he'd be going against. When Connie Hawkins first came to the Lakers last year, he brought a cassette player into the locker room so he could listen to music before the games. Players on a lot of teams do this, but it bothered Jerry and he asked the Hawk if he'd mind not bringing the cassette player with him. Connie left it home after that.

As we walked through the tunnel leading to the court, I

stood back against the wall for a minute and let everybody else go by. I looked at the new faces—Zelmo Beaty and Brian Winters and Cazzie Russell, who was standing out near our bench on crutches—and I realized how nice it felt to be there, starting another year of pro basketball. Then I ran out onto the floor and started taking a few shots.

Pretty soon I heard a few whistles and I started to smile. When I was in high school a whole group of us practiced this strange high-pitched whistle that carries over great distances. It sounds sort of like squeaky brakes going down a hill. The whistle originated with just a small group of us, but there are hundreds of people who know it now. When I went to college, I didn't have much contact with my friends in Los Angeles because I couldn't afford phone calls, never was much of a letter writer, and didn't get down here much. But if we were in town to play UCLA or Southern California, my friends would come out, and as soon as my team appeared on the floor I'd hear the whistle. I would look around and there would be six or eight guys standing halfway up in the stands waving their arms and whistling. Today, when my friends can't afford to buy a ticket down near the floor, they just give me the whistle from the $5 seats up in the rafters. It sounded like there were a lot of them there tonight.

It's fun to play in the town where you grew up because there is always somebody around you know. Tonight I got a kick out of just acknowledging everybody's presence as I stood in the warmup lines waiting to get the ball. Once, as I went by to drive to the basket, John Ramsay, the Lakers' public address broadcaster, put on his deep announcer's voice and I overheard him begin the introductions, without a mike of course, "And from Morningside High School here in Inglewood . . . Stan Love." It sounded so good to me that I unintentionally missed the layup.

The game started off well. Pat Riley did a good job guarding Rick Barry and we ran with the Warriors pretty well. Golden State likes to fast-break a lot, and that's what we're going to have to do this year too. We've got to get the ball off the boards, beat the other team down the floor, and get a good shot. Which is not as easy as it sounds.

We were up by five points a[...]
about two minutes into the second p[...]
Winters, and I all went in. We played t[...]
and increased the lead to 12 points at the[...]
nice feeling. The second-stringers pride the[...]
ing things even if the team is ahead, and here w[...]
pulling further in front. Everybody was playing
especially Brian, who looked just great for a rookie
league game. At one point Rick Barry gave me a c[...] or
moves and then pulled up for a 20-foot jump shot that was
good. As we were going back the other way, Rick was guarding
me as I came off a pick and took a pass from Gail Goodrich.
I gave him a fake and shot a 20-footer that was good. Almost
exactly the same play. It wasn't intentional, like "Now it's my
turn," but it nullified his basket and I will be happy any time
I can nullify a Rick Barry score.

Our group got back in at the end of the third quarter too,
with about the same results. I guess Bill must have been
happy. I felt pretty confident on defense, and once, as Clifford
Ray, the Warriors' center, was going up for a dunk shot, he
brought the ball back over his head and I sort of popped it out
of his hands from behind. Ray didn't even know he had lost the
ball, and he followed through into the basket with two hands
full of nothing.

We won the game 105–90, and everybody felt very good.
To play that well after all our problems was really encouraging. There was an air of excitement in the locker room because
we knew that to get into the playoffs we'd have to beat Golden
State consistently. Maybe this victory would give them something to think about.

Mimeographed box scores of the game were passed
around in the locker room, and I saw that I had played 22
minutes and scored ten points. Gail had 34 points and Jim
Price had 21, so it was our backcourt shooters who were doing
most of the scoring. But the best part from my point of view
was that Pat and I had held Rick Barry to 14 points, which is
almost nothing for him. Then I saw something else on the box
score that made me wince. Connie Hawkins hadn't played.

minute. I looked over at him and could almost
pain in his eyes.

fterward, a lot of my family and friends were waiting for
me at the entrance to the tunnel outside the Forum. We
walked out to the car to talk for a while. Everybody was very
animated and happy. As we were talking, the Hawk came out
and my niece Marie, who is 12, asked him for his autograph.
He signed it but didn't say anything, and then he walked on.
Normally, he'd stop and chat for a minute.

"What's wrong with Connie Hawkins?" Marie asked me.

"It's kind of hard to explain, honey," I told her. I knew
exactly how he felt, but there was no way she would understand.

OCTOBER 19

"I can see you're going to be impossible today," Cheryl said.

"Who, me?" I said as I sat down to start in on the big
breakfast she had just made. Actually, considering what time
it was, I guess it was really brunch. "Now why would you say
a thing like that about Mr. Nice Guy?"

"Take a look at the papers, Mr. Nice Guy," she said.

"Oh, yeah?" I said, and I reached for the *Herald-Examiner* to see what Rich Levin had written. Rich is a friend of
mine and lives nearby. His wife, Susan, is very close to Cheryl.
Rich used to play the game a little. In fact, his greatest claim
to fame is that he sat on the bench at UCLA when the Bruins
won their first two NCAA titles in 1964 and 1965. The twelfth
man on 12-man teams, which nobody ever lets him forget.

"Stan Love," he wrote, "has apparently convinced his
coach he wants to play." Good, Rich, good. I wonder if Bill
Sharman reads the *Herald-Examiner?*

In the *Times* Dwight Chapin said, "Stan Love rebounded aggressively and looked like a man who wants to—and could —become a starter."

He noticed. How nice. Cheryl's right. I'm going to be impossible today.

OCTOBER 20

It doesn't take much for that good optimistic feeling to disappear. One loss usually does it. And that's what we had presented to us tonight by the Kansas City–Omaha Kings. Coaches often like to talk about team victories. Well, this was a team defeat. The problems were everywhere. The Kings' guards, Nate Archibald and Jimmy Walker, killed us, not only from the floor but also on the foul line. Between them they made 15 free throws, and as a team the Kings were 29 of 36 from the foul line, while we were 15 of 20. We actually scored more from the floor than they did, but there isn't much you can do when they're shooting free throws all night. Walker ended up with 27 points and Archibald had 20; Gail Goodrich and Jim Price had only 27 between them. The only bright spot for us was Pat Riley, who scored 30 points. But as a whole we played a sloppy game and lost by ten points.

I was nothing to brag about myself, although I guess eight points in 14 minutes is respectable offensively. I was guarding Nate Williams, who is only 6-5 but is quick and strong as a football player. I found it hard to stop him and he got nine points in the nine minutes he played. The Kings just about blew us out in the second quarter—and led 55–48 at the half —but we came back to tie it in the third period. Then Archibald just took control and they won easily. We all felt pretty bad because a team like the Kings shouldn't beat us going away like that. When it happens, it makes you wonder.

Bill Sharman was angry after the game. He said we practiced shitty yesterday and we played like we practiced. Maybe somebody should kick him in the ass for letting us scrimmage the way we did, he said. If guys didn't want to practice, didn't want to run up and down, he said, we should let him know and he'd work something out. It sounded like he was saying that if a player didn't feel good, he'd excuse him from practice, but it also had a sort of threatening ring to it. Especially after what he said about Connie Hawkins yesterday.

When a reporter asked Bill why the Hawk hadn't played in the first game, he said, "He won't play until he wants to fast-break and run from one end of the court to the other." Which is kind of a rough thing to read about yourself in the papers. Connie didn't play again tonight and I'd think that his attitude might be a little different from what it was two nights ago. It's one thing when you don't play and the team looks good and wins. But it's something else when you don't play and the team looks bad and loses. Then you might have the right to think the club could have won if you'd been allowed to play. But it might be that Bill's strategy is working a little. Connie seems to be getting into it a little more in practice. He was working hard against Pat Riley yesterday and even warming up hard, which is unusual for him.

One defeat doesn't tell us anything about ourselves—any more than the one win over the Warriors did. But I sense a different kind of feeling on the club this season. You hear guys mutter that it's not the way it used to be. Maybe it was the loss of Jerry West—the last superstar from the Chamberlain-Baylor-West days—that did it, but the feeling now seems to be that we are just another ball club that will have to scramble and fight for everything we get. It will no longer be enough just to *be* the Los Angeles Lakers. We're going to have to *play* like the Lakers, and that may not be easy. I know Bill recognizes it. He told the press the other day that we can no longer simply overpower teams. Now we have to play competitively because in terms of talent we're no longer that much better than other teams. It's still very early, though. We'll just have to see how it all shakes down.

OCTOBER 23

As we were getting dressed for practice today, I got on Frank O'Neill a little bit about the parking situation at the Loyola gym. There are very few spaces around the building itself and most are filled when we get there. I parked on the street the other day and got a ticket, so I told Frank that if he'd pull his car in a little more I'd be able to squeeze in behind him.

"Yeah, Frank," said Gail Goodrich, "why don't you do that? Why don't you get us some parking around here? If I get a ticket I'm not paying it."

Gail was so wrought up about it that you could almost predict what would happen next. Someone just couldn't resist the opportunity to mess with him a little.

"Sure, Gail," one of the guys said. "Your ass will be in jail if you don't pay your ticket. They'll tow your car away and prosecute you."

"If Loyola University wants to lock me up because of a parking ticket," Gail said, "I will just have Pete Newell come down and get me out."

"Don't worry about it, Gail," I said. "I'll come down and get you out. We need those ten points a game."

Everybody kind of went "Ooooo," and Gail looked at me and burst out laughing. "All right," he said, "you got me."

It isn't all that funny, of course. From 34 points in the first game Gail fell off to 10 against the Kings and was only 3 for 16 from the floor. The way we're set up, it might be OK for some guys to be hot one night and cold the next because somebody else might take up the slack. But if Gail doesn't score every time out, we're in a lot of trouble. He has to get those 20 points a game, and if he gets shut off or has to struggle for them we'll be struggling too. Last season, when he had to do it for the first time without Jerry West, Gail really had problems in some games. But then he'd snap out of it and start hitting again. Once, against Portland, he scored 49 points, his career high.

It's hard to see outward signs of how this consistent pressure affects Gail. After the Kansas City game you could sense how upset he was, but there was no emotion on his face. The next day at practice it was like nothing had happened; he was out there working hard and trying to forget his bad night. It's really an amazing attitude and I admire Gail for it.

While we were getting taped, Elmore Smith told me that Al Ross had been sitting in the front row during the first two games and he'd told the Lakers to get Ross out of there. Ross is one of the top business managers in sports—he's negotiated a lot of the big contracts you read about—but he and Elmore have had a falling out and are suing each other. In fact, Ross is having trouble with other clients of his, Spencer Haywood for example. Anyway, his presence up in the front row, practically sitting on the court, has Elmore bummed out. The Lakers told him that if it happens again they'll get Ross out of there.

Just before we went out on the floor, Bill Bridges called out, "Hey, Frank, who are you making up the new uniform for?" Everybody looked around sort of startled and Frank said, "I'm not making up a new uniform."

There were a few laughs at Bridges' little joke. Then Pat Riley said, "Well, it's back to the pines for me." I wondered what the hell he could be talking about. How could they bench a guy who had just scored 30 points? But Pat has a good feel for what's going on so I guess it's possible. The real surprise came later, though: for a few minutes at the end of practice I was working out with the gold squad—with Gail, Jim, Elmore, and Happy Hairston. I wish I knew what was in Bill Sharman's mind. Is he thinking of starting me?

OCTOBER 25

Cazzie Russell showed up at the shootaround this morning and seemed to be in a remarkably good state of mind. He has taken his injury philosophically and is working hard on rehabilitating his knee. Of course, he can't train much with a cast from his ankle to his knee, but he's doing what they tell him to. He even put his crutches down for a few minutes and took some shooting practice. He looked pretty strange out there trying to balance himself on the cast, but he made a good percentage of his shots. The Lakers took some pictures of him working out to send around to the papers.

Cazzie has his recuperation schedule written out on his cast and it isn't very promising. He doesn't get out of the cast until December 6, and he can't even start jogging till after Christmas. By January 10 he'll be allowed to run, and he's supposed to be back playing by January 17. He says he's hoping to beat the timetable and be back sooner, but I don't know. I'll be surprised if he plays much at all this year.

I should explain, by the way, that a shootaround is a Bill Sharman invention. On the morning or afternoon of a game he likes to get us out to the court to take a little shooting practice just to get the feel of the court and prepare for the game we'll be playing that night. I don't know whether players in other sports practice the day of the game—except for a little loosening up just before the game starts—but a lot of NBA teams have picked up on it. The reason might be that Bill instituted it the year the Lakers won 33 straight games and the title. Many other coaches have·been doing it ever since.

The game against Detroit tonight had all the earmarks of a runaway win for us. We'd been off for five days and the Pistons, who haven't yet played a game at home, have been traveling all over the country for the last week. So when we went up 62–46 at the half, we figured we had a lock on it. But we lost by three points.

It was horrible. We didn't keep the pressure on them in the third quarter, and all of a sudden they were just coming at us and coming at us; it seemed like there was nothing we could do. The tempo of the game just swung over to their side. Once a team gets hot, everything it does seems to work. And with guys like Dave Bing, Bob Lanier, and Curtis Rowe the Pistons can get hot in a hurry. Also, teams seem to get sky high when they play in Los Angeles or New York. The crowds are good, it's a nice new arena, and you're playing against a traditionally good team. The visiting teams seem to put out a little extra in the Forum, and if you let up on them you're in trouble.

Connie Hawkins got into his first game of the season—12 minutes, two points—and my playing time fell off to six minutes. I don't understand it. I just have no idea what Bill is doing any more. This loss really bothered him, and he kept the locker room closed for 15 minutes after the game. He likes to regain his composure before he meets with the press. He gets so intense and angry when we lose that he needs time to cool himself off.

He kept us sitting on our stools for about five minutes, telling us what we'd done wrong—that we'd gotten killed on the boards and hurt on defense and had made too many turnovers. Bill never yells at us—he's had serious voice problems the last few years from yelling at the referees too much—but keeps things on as businesslike a level as he can. He tries not to get emotional and sometimes he sounds as if he's only critiquing a practice session. But you can tell he's fuming, and what he'd probably like to do is to take a few guys in the back room and beat the shit out of them.

OCTOBER 27

Anybody need a 25-year-old, 6-9, 210-pound forward? Have sweat suit, will travel. A willing worker, and the price is right.

It happened like this. We played Phoenix in the Forum tonight. We were doing reasonably well in the first half, especially after Zelmo Beaty came off the bench and started hitting his soft little jump shot from eight or ten feet out. Happy Hairston, Bill Bridges, and Pat Riley were doing a nice job defensively and on the boards. So since the front line was performing well I didn't have anything to complain about when I didn't play in the first half. We led at halftime 55–47.

Then the second half started and we blew the Suns out. We scored the first 13 points of the third quarter and led 68–47. The game is over. Now it's strictly what Chick Hearn likes to call garbage time. Everybody gets in and takes a little shooting practice. And everybody did. Except Connie Hawkins and me. About halfway through the period, as the lead got bigger and bigger, a few fans started chanting, "We want the Hawk! We want the Hawk!" After a few minutes it seemed like everyone in the building was into it.

Connie was really digging it. He was smiling and looking all around, stretching one of his long arms behind the bench and making an upward motion with his hand as if to say, "More, more." Well, that brought the house down. People were really screaming and yelling and not paying any attention to the game.

"Hey, Hawk," I said. "Don't go in without me. Make this a package deal."

"OK, man," said Connie, who was having such a good

time I thought he might stand up and take a bow.

The period went on and I figured I'd get in at the start of the fourth quarter. But no, Bill Sharman came down the bench to the Hawk and said, "Connie, would you like to play tonight?" And there I was sitting next to him thinking, Shit, why don't you ask *me* if *I* would like to play tonight? But the Hawk went into the game and Bill just walked back to the other end of the bench and sat down again.

I figured perhaps I'd get in with ten minutes left . . . and then maybe with eight minutes left . . . and then maybe with six minutes left. I started thinking about my family and friends again, about my little sister who had brought two friends, what they must be thinking about my not playing when we were ahead by more than 20 points.

Finally, with four minutes to go, I heard Bill call my name. I sat there for a minute, thinking, Why? But then I got up, walked down to the end of the bench, sat down, and started taking off my sweat pants.

"Bill," I said as I stood up, "I think this is a pretty shitty deal."

He looked at me kind of funny for a minute and then said, "Well, you can go back and sit down then." Which I did. I watched the rest of the game from my chair.

Bill didn't say anything after the game, but everybody on the team saw what happened and they weren't about to let it pass.

"What happened with you and the man?" somebody asked.

Bill Bridges said, "Everybody goes through the young rebellious ballplayer bit. I did the same thing."

Happy Hairston stood around saying, "Oh, Stanley. Oh, Stanley."

Finally, I looked over at Connie and just had to laugh. "What happened to our package deal?" I said.

"Hey, man," the Hawk said, "when the man called me, all I could think was, Fuck you, Love."

"Thanks a lot, Hawk," I said. It was nice not to be uptight about it. I just wonder what Bill thinks.

On the way home Cheryl and I discussed it. "Can't you just go in and talk to the guy like we are talking now?" she said.

"No, it's not like that. You just can't do it. They have something in their minds about how they are going to run things and if you are part of it, that's great. But if you're not, there is really not much you can do about it. You can just stick with it and keep working. But that's all."

When we got home we lit a fire, had some dinner, and sat around drinking a little wine and listening to music. After a while we started making notes of the things I should and shouldn't have done. I should have stayed cool. I should have gone into the game when he said to and discussed it with him later. I shouldn't have been so negative because the season is young and nothing has really been decided yet. It all made a lot of sense. I only wish I believed it was true.

OCTOBER 28

On the flight up to Portland today I kept pretty much to myself. I didn't want to get into anything with Bill Sharman in front of the other players. I hope we can get a chance to talk about what happened, but I'd prefer privacy. So I just sat in my seat and thought about how much had happened since I'd been traded to the Lakers.

I was tremendously frustrated after my second season in Baltimore. I couldn't see where staying with the Bullets was leading me. So before I left for home, I went in to see Gene Shue to ask him to trade me. I never got the chance.

"Stan," he said, "there is really not that much of a future for you here in the system I run, so this summer we're going to try to make a deal for you."

I tried not to let him know how happy I was to hear that, but I don't think I succeeded. When nothing happened all summer, though, I figured the Bullets hadn't been able to make a deal for me—or hadn't tried—and that I'd be back in Baltimore in the fall. Just thinking about it made me grouchy. But late in August I was sitting around at home when the phone rang. It was Bob Ferry, the Bullets' general manager.

"Stan," he said, "I just traded you to Los Angeles."

I looked at the clock—it must have been midnight in the East—and all I could think was, What is he doing calling so late? He sounded like he was drunk. And, for an incredibly long time, I didn't believe him.

"Don't bullshit me, Bob," I said. "It's not even funny. I'm trying to get myself together to come back to Baltimore." (It takes a lot of getting together to go to Baltimore.) "I'm tired of not playing for you guys for two years. I am coming back and I am getting myself ready to go at it again."

"No, no," he said. "I'm serious. I just made the deal myself. I just got off the phone with them and they'll be calling you in a few minutes. We could have traded you to a couple of other teams, but we knew you wanted to be out west."

How touching, I thought to myself. And then it hit me. He was telling me the *truth*. I *had* been traded. To the *Lakers*. I was stunned. Finally, I managed to thank him and he wished me well, told me that he wanted me to make it, that he knew I could and that I should work on my attitude a little bit. At last, I hung up the phone and all I could think was, I'm going to the Lakers. I'm going to the Lakers. To tell you the truth, I cried. I remembered when I was in Morningside High School and they were building the Forum just a couple of blocks away. I would ride my motorcycle down the utility ramp and park near the construction site, wondering what it would be like to be a professional basketball player. And now I would be playing there. My family and friends could see me play.

Pretty soon Pete Newell called and said how glad the Lakers were to have me, how they had tried to draft me out of college. Would I like to come over to the Lakers' office to get acquainted the next day, and would I like to go to a sports luncheon in the San Fernando Valley later in the week? The high I was on seemed to last for days; it was like a dream you don't wake up from. It seemed as if the phone never stopped ringing, as if everybody in the world was as happy and excited as I was. Out on tour, the Beach Boys sent me a telegram: "Congratulations to the newest Laker from the oldest rock and roll group."

OCTOBER 29

I was in my hotel room before the game with Portland tonight when the phone rang. It was Bill Sharman.

"Come on down to my room," he said. "I want to kick around a few things with you."

I put down what I was reading: four handwritten, legal-sized pages Steve had given me before the flight up here yesterday. I'd left the notes Cheryl and I had made Sunday night on the bar in the living room and Steve had seen them. He had elaborated on them, writing down a bunch of things I should tell Bill if I got the chance.

He wrote about how hard I'd worked all summer to get into shape, how good I'd looked in the exhibition season, how I'd done pretty well in the first few games, and how my playing time had gone down anyway. He even wrote that I should tell Bill that if he didn't plan on using me perhaps he should trade me.

I'm really ambivalent about that. It would be hard leaving my family and friends, but I'm still in the learning stage and sometimes I think what I need is to go to a team where they will say, "You've got 30 minutes a game for four months to learn this game. If you can't do it in that time, you're on your way out." Steve also said I should tell Bill I didn't mean to upset him by not going into the Phoenix game, but that I had to let him know I didn't want to be used only in garbage-time situations and that I hoped he had more respect for me as a ballplayer than that.

I'd read what he'd written three or four times when Bill called, but I left the notes in my room when I went down to see him. When I walked in and saw that he had a list of notes too, I had to laugh.

"I didn't bring mine," I said, pointing at his papers. "Can I go get them?"

Bill smiled and put his notes aside and we just talked. I was happy and relieved to see that he didn't seem to be mad about my little tantrum. He went over a lot of the same old stuff, about working on defense and having a good attitude. It seemed as if he wanted to encourage me more than anything else.

I apologized for what I'd done and he said he could understand it, that if a player didn't get upset when he didn't play he'd wonder what was wrong with him. "On the one hand, it's good that you got involved and got upset," he said, "but on the other hand, you have to learn to control it. You probably thought I put Connie in the game ahead of you because the fans were yelling for him."

"I only wondered why I couldn't play when we were 21 points ahead," I said.

"I was doing a few new things," he said, "trying to get Connie started."

We talked for quite a while and finally I got around to the question of my future with the Lakers. I said that as far as my career is concerned, I could feel myself becoming a better player, developing and learning, and that what I need is the playing time. Maybe it would be better, I said, if I could go to a team where I could play more. It certainly wasn't a threat, because I'm hardly in a position to threaten anybody, but I was glad I'd said it. Bill didn't really answer me, but I think he took it the way I meant it and not as implying I wasn't willing to do everything I could to help the team.

I left Bill's room in an exceptionally good mood. I'd said everything I'd wanted to say and we seemed to understand each other better than before. I was in such a good mood, in fact, that I didn't even get mad when I didn't play tonight against Portland.

Maybe it was because we won 105–102. Bill Bridges clinched it when he stole the ball from Sidney Wicks as he was going in for a layup at the end of the game. Elmore Smith and Zelmo Beaty did a good job on Bill Walton, who got only 12 points. Our front line didn't produce much, but Jim Price and Gail Goodrich each had 23 and that saved us as far as scoring was concerned.

Why didn't I play? Who knows? Maybe Bill wanted to make a point of it with the other ballplayers. But it really didn't bother me. I feel that things will get better for me as the season progresses.

OCTOBER 30

I have never seen Bill Sharman this upset. It seemed like he was in a state of shock. He just sat in a chair, stared at the wall, and sipped a beer. I think it's the second time I have ever seen him drink beer. He acted like he had been hit by a truck and didn't know where he was. Actually, we were the ones who were hit by the truck. Seattle ran us down tonight 117–97. It was just a slaughter. And by a team we should *beat* by 20 points.

Part of the problem was that the SuperSonics were just unreal. They simply didn't miss. Hell, they had 70 points in the first half and they must have shot 70 percent. Even with only 47 points in the second half, they ended up making over half their shots for the game. But there was more to it than that. The problems with our front line were never more evident, and the guards couldn't make up the difference as far as scoring was concerned. The Seattle starting forwards—Spencer Haywood and Leonard Gray—outshot Happy Hairston and Pat Riley, our starters, 64–9. In the first half they outshot them 39–0. Pat didn't score a point. Bill Bridges played a lot and got 15 points, but he couldn't contain Haywood either. I got in for 20 minutes and scored nine points, but Gray acted like I wasn't there. Of course, by then the Sonics knew they had us, and with no pressure they just kept gunning—and hitting.

After he finished his beer, Bill looked around the room and started talking about the game. There wasn't much he could say, though, and pretty soon he asked for comments, which he likes to do from time to time. Zelmo Beaty spoke and everybody sort of perked up. Zelmo commands a lot of respect because of the solid image he projects. He has this nice little shot he likes to take from eight or ten feet out, but that doesn't fool anybody. His game is strength and he's good at it. When Zelmo gets the ball, it's his ball. Nobody *ever* tears it out of his hands. Zelmo doesn't say a lot in team meetings, but when he does it's because he has something to say and everybody listens.

Zelmo said he didn't think the problems with the front line were entirely the fault of the big men, that part of them rested with the guards. He said if the guards would give the ball up a little more, it would put more pressure on the opposing forwards to guard us. Since they knew we weren't going to get the ball much, they didn't have to worry about us and could concentrate on scoring. All they had to do was screen us out, get the rebound, and go down and play offense. If there were more pressure on them when we had the ball, they would score less.

Zelmo's point was that the guards should quarterback the team more—try to develop a balanced scoring attack—instead of worrying only about shooting. The guards should come down the court and try to penetrate—put pressure on the defense by dribbling and passing—and draw the defenders out toward them. Then they could pass off to the guy who had an open shot, whether it's another guard, a forward, or the center.

In a way, Zelmo was right. We've got to get everybody involved, get everybody shooting, so the defense has a lot to worry about. Now all the forwards seem to do is set screens for the guards, who dribble off them and shoot jump shots. The guards do the shooting, Happy does the rebounding, and the big center clogs up the middle. That's a fine system for the old West-Chamberlain-Baylor Lakers, but we're not that kind of team any more. We have to tailor our offense to the people we've got. And we simply must play more as a team.

Except for the teams that have an outstanding superstar, it seems to me that the best basketball teams are just that: the best *teams*. But there's a built-in problem when it comes to getting players to think that way. Everybody on the court can be a star. Everyone can shoot, can score, can play his man one on one and dazzle the fans with his great moves. There are so many individual egos in the game that it can be difficult to create a close-knit group playing as a unit.

It's not the same as football, where, say, the offensive line knows that its only job is to block and there is very little chance of getting the adulation that goes to the quarterback or the running back or the pass receiver. And the plays are called one at a time, with each man given a certain responsibility on each one. Baseball is different too, because on offense each player gets his chance to be a star in turn while everybody else stands and watches. But basketball is more of a free-lance game where things happen almost spontaneously much of the time and anybody can try to do almost anything. It takes an unselfish, disciplined player not at least to *think* of shooting when he has the ball. Team play can be very hard to instill. And we seem to be moving backward at times. Even last year there seemed to be better five-man play on the Lakers than we've shown so far, more movement with the ball, more involvement by everybody on the floor.

There was no big discussion of what Zelmo said, but I hope it sinks in. It makes a lot of sense to me.

81

Footnote on tonight's game: Connie Hawkins did not play. This is where we came in.

NOVEMBER 1

We beat Milwaukee tonight at the Forum 109–86. Normally, that would be cause for rejoicing, but under the circumstances it is no big thing. The circumstances are that Kareem Abdul-Jabbar is home with a scratched eyeball and injured finger. With him, the Bucks are as good a team as there is in the league. Without him, they're less than mediocre. They've played half a dozen games now and only won one.

Before the game I talked with Terry Driscoll of the Bucks —we played together in Baltimore—and he said that without Abdul-Jabbar it was just a different game. It's amazing how important he is to the team, Terry said. Watching them play, I could see what he means. They seemed to be dragging from the start, just going through the motions without any life or enthusiasm. Except for their coach, Larry Costello. He was quite excited, running up and down the court, yelling and exhorting his players all the time. Several of the Lakers commented that it must be difficult to play for a coach who yells so much.

While I was talking to Terry, I remembered my own brief encounter with Kareem—he was Lew Alcindor then—and my quick lesson in the way he dominates any game he's in. It was my sophomore year at Oregon, and UCLA came to Eugene to play us. Alcindor was a senior then, and our coach, Steve Belko, had been going crazy for three years trying to stop him and the Bruins. He hadn't had any more success at it than anybody else, of course. One year, in its first game against

UCLA, Oregon got beaten 100–66, so when the two teams met again a short time later Belko tried a stall. It worked in a way: UCLA only won 34–25.

For us, Belko's plan was to guard Alcindor as little as possible so he wouldn't get mad. The idea was not to upset him so he'd get pissed and score 35 points and destroy us. We just wanted to contain him, sort of bore him with the game. At that point in his career, as a matter of fact, Lew was easily bored. The NCAA had outlawed dunking the ball, just because of him, and that took a lot of the spirit out of the game as far as he was concerned. Also, he'd already been on two national championship teams and was well on his way to a third. The college game just wasn't a challenge to him any more. He knew he was on his way to the pros, he knew he was worth a lot of money and he knew Oregon didn't mean shit to him.

I couldn't believe the casualness with which he played. He seemed to be in a daze the whole game, just cruising, in second gear almost. We were very careful to let him do what he wanted, not to try to beat him up or steal the ball from him, so he wouldn't get excited. I guarded him and I certainly didn't want to get into a physical thing with him. I just tried subtly to get my points and some good rebounds and at the same time try not to aggravate him. It seemed to work because of the lackadaisical way he played, but when it was over he had 27 points to my 18 and it certainly didn't have any effect on the game. He killed us 93–64.

The few times I've played against Abdul-Jabbar in the NBA, it's been entirely different. It's his *job* now, and he comes to play every night. His emotion is much higher. And when you add that to his height and his incredible ability— well, he's the best there is. What else can you say? The Bucks are in serious trouble without him.

My only contribution to the win over Milwaukee tonight was five points in five minutes of garbage time. I was mad, of course, but I didn't think of repeating my pouting act. In fact, when Bill Sharman called me up to his end of the bench to go in, we kind of giggled at each other. He knew how I felt and said, "Just go in there and work on things."

I'm beginning to get the idea this is going to be a very long season.

NOVEMBER 2

We had the day off today—no game, no practice—and Elmore Smith and Brian Winters came over to the house for lunch. Afterward, we went for a walk on the beach and threw around a football and a Frisbee. I even got into a volleyball game with Steve for a few minutes, which is something I really shouldn't do during the season. When you're concentrating on one sport, it's not a good idea to play another one. The three of us talked about the team and the league and some of the players, the whole basketball scene, but we really didn't get into the Lakers' situation very much. Elmore seems a little bugged about the way things are going. His knee is hurting him again along with both his ankles. And he's got a cold. I left him alone.

Sometimes, just before games, I'll get on Elmore and tell him to play really hard in the first quarter. "Just go out and go wild and kill them," I'll tell him. "Just establish yourself. These guys get off on you when they think it's easy. Don't let them do that. Don't let them think they can come in and make layups and close jumpers on you. Make them pay for it." Sometimes it seems to help and sometimes it doesn't.

I often think he doesn't realize how important he is to the Lakers. He could be so dominant. You see it sometimes when he's out there killing people on the boards, blocking shots and making dunks. If only he would do it consistently. Part of the problem might be the pressure on him. Nobody ever says, "Elmore, it's your fault," when we lose, but that's always sort of an undercurrent. In the NBA you generally rap your center when you're not going well because it is the key position. The entire offense and defense are dependent on him.

Another thing is that Elmore is still very young in terms of experience. He turns the wrong way sometimes, gets caught, and corrects himself a split second too late. These are the kinds of things only playing time will help. I think the Lakers really have to go easy with him. But they're not used to that. They expect high quality performance immediately and are even more demanding when they're losing.

NOVEMBER 3

At the morning shootaround before our game with Buffalo tonight Connie Hawkins looked around and called out, "Hey, where's Weird?"

"Yeah, where's Happy?" somebody else shouted over to Frank O'Neill.

"He's got McAdooitis," Frank hollered back. "Bad."

Everybody cracked up. Actually, Happy is pretty sick—he had two flu shots—but nobody can be thrilled about having to play against Bob McAdoo. He's burning up the league and is a major reason why Buffalo has improved so much this year. McAdoo is 6-10—below average for a center—but he's so incredibly quick that no center can guard him, certainly not Elmore Smith or Zelmo Beaty. You almost always have to put a forward on him, and even that doesn't stop him from getting 25 to 30 points a game. Or more.

The game tonight was unbelievable. Embarrassing is a better word, I guess. Buffalo outscored us 40–16 in the first quarter, and they should have called the game then. If it had been a chess match we'd have resigned. Everybody just went through the motions for the next three periods, and the Braves ended up winning 124–101. McAdoo had 32.

It's interesting how well the Braves have developed with the addition of McAdoo and Jim McMillian. Ernie DiGregorio, who scored so well as a rookie last year, is out for a while with a knee injury, and I've heard some people say his absence might actually help Buffalo because he's weak on defense. Last year they were calling him Ernie No D instead of Ernie D. But I think it's a bad rap. He'll develop defensively as he gets experience and he more than compensates on offense. He's a very unselfish player and creates a lot of scoring situations with his passing, as well as being a fine shot.

It was sad to see how we struggled against the Braves. There wasn't even an attempt at team play after a while. The guards just came down and tried to shoot over the men guarding them. Jim Price, in particular, was really forcing shots. Elmore missed a couple of easy shots early in the game and pretty soon the fans were booing him and cheering when Zelmo finally replaced him. As for the forwards, it was more of the same. Happy played only five minutes because he was feeling so lousy, and Pat Riley, the other starter, scored 12 points playing about half the game. Bill Bridges and Connie Hawkins had only seven points between them. I had ten points playing 16 minutes at the end when it was pretty much just shooting practice because the score was so lopsided.

You try to guard against it, of course, but it's easy to develop bad habits when you play only in garbage-time situations. When you're hopelessly behind, nobody really wants to get in and mix it up under the boards or try to change the flow. By the time I entered the game, Buffalo had replaced McAdoo with Dale Schlueter, who's noted for putting people out with injuries. At one point he almost butchered Zelmo to stop him from scoring, and who the hell wants to get beat up like that in a hopeless situation? By then it doesn't matter how well you play, so you just try to hustle as best you can, grab a few rebounds, score a few points, play good defense. You pick your spots rather than really going all out.

Even when your team is still in the game, coming off the bench can be difficult. You're cold when you go in, and a favorite tactic of opposing teams is to run three or four plays right at you because you're not ready. Now you're stiff and you're trying to impress the coach, and a lot of times you find yourself committing a foul right away because you're not in the tempo of the game. That's one thing I really have to work on. Last year, when I'd come in and foul a guy, Chick Hearn would get very upset. Once he called me the biggest fouler in the league and implied I'd lost a game for us because of a foul. My father was listening to the game and told me later he felt like jumping in his car and driving down to choke Chick. I laughed when he told me that because Dad is really a very mild guy on the surface, but he is an intense man inside. I guess the fans can get wound up in the game as much as the players sometimes.

Poor Bill Sharman. He just can't understand what is happening with us, why we're so inconsistent. How can we look so good in one game and then get killed in the next? I looked around the locker room after the game, trying to detach myself and be objective about it, but I couldn't figure it out either. Potentially, we have a good team. But I just don't know whether we're intelligent enough, or unselfish enough, to come together to win. Something has got to happen, whether it's a trade or a change in the lineup or whatever. It's fascinating to go to practice to see what's going on.

There has been one bright spot lately: our foul shooting. We were 19 for 22 tonight, 23 for 25 against Milwaukee, 27 for 28 at Seattle, and 25 for 28 at Portland. One of the reporters mentioned it to Bill tonight and he said, "Yeah, but don't forget that I am the guy who taught Wilt Chamberlain everything he knows about foul shooting."

Wilt was, of course, just about the worst free-throw shooter in the history of the game.

NOVEMBER 4

I don't know what to take first: the pills, the cough syrup, or the vitamins. I can still feel the effects of the antibiotics they pumped into my ass and it was all I could do to get through practice today. It's my first cold of the season and probably not my last. Basketball players get them all the time. It's the change in temperatures and the travel, I think. You go from the West Coast, where it's warm, back to the East, where you're moving from hot arenas and hotels out into the snow and cold. You're keeping funny hours, eating irregularly, changing time zones, sleeping sporadically. It can get to you after a while.

In truth, nobody on the Lakers is feeling too well these days. We're all upset because we just don't seem to be able to put it together. Splitting our first eight games has already put us two and a half games behind the Warriors and it's starting to get to us. Bill Sharman is holding longer practices, trying to figure out working combinations, but the scrimmages have been raggedy. Nobody's really hustling as hard as he could. Everybody seems to be waiting for something to happen.

Another thing is that the crowds at the Forum haven't been very good lately. I think part of it has to do with Jerry West's retiring; he was very popular with the fans. But also we're not winning, and that's the biggest factor. With ticket prices the way they are, we simply have to win to get people to come out. Nobody is going to spend $8.75 to watch a two-hour basketball game if his team is getting killed. The cheapest seat you can buy at the Forum costs $5 and you're so far away you need to use a good pair of binoculars.

The building holds 17,505 for basketball, and when the Lakers were on their way to the NBA title three years ago, they filled it regularly. Lately, they've been announcing crowds of between 10,000 and 12,000, but you can tell there aren't that many people there. They count season tickets as part of the paid attendance whether the people who bought them are there or not. So some nights the place is barely half full even though a respectable number of tickets have been sold.

The attitude of the fans is different too. We hear some booing now and it's hard not to be aware of it. I know we're supposed to be professionals and not pay any attention to that, but you can't help being concerned when your own fans seem to be hardening their attitude against you and expecting you to lose.

The unsettled nature of the situation has all the forwards on edge. It seems that we are openly joking all the time about changes just to relieve nervous tension. Bill Bridges is constantly mentioning possibilities. Bob Love lost his appeal to the commissioner over his salary dispute with Chicago so now he has to decide whether to play with the Bulls or not. He could still be traded, I guess. Our biggest problem is that the forwards just aren't scoring. We're certainly not holding our own against the Rick Barrys and the Bob McAdoos, the guys who are going to get their points every time out. Why doesn't Bill put a guy in there who can do some shooting, who can score back? I could suggest someone he could use a little more.

NOVEMBER 5

Elmore Smith and I were walking out of the Loyola gym after practice today when he said, "Did you know about ——— and ———?" He mentioned the names of two guys who had played for the Lakers a few years ago.

"What do you mean?" I said.

"One of the reasons they were traded," he said, "was that they were accused of being a bad influence on the team because they smoked grass."

"No shit," I said.

"Well, that's the talk."

I started thinking about it and I wondered if maybe it wasn't just a good excuse for management to get rid of a guy because he wasn't helping the team much. In other words, the reasoning is this: "He doesn't get back on defense, he can't learn our system, and besides that he gets high." It's all just hearsay, of course, but nervousness about this sort of thing does surface from time to time.

When I first came to the Lakers, I was sitting next to Jim Price in the locker room and he told me it was wise not to say a lot about your personal life. He said there were some guys who liked to talk in the front office about other ballplayers. It's to be expected, I guess. There must be people like that on every team. I have no idea whether it's true or not, but I can see that the fact some guys *think* it's true may be one reason for the withdrawn, closed-mouth attitude on the part of many of the Lakers. Jim told me that it started with Wilt Chamberlain—for a different reason. "Wilt brought that whole be-careful-what-you-say thing to the Lakers," Jim said, "because he got paranoid about everything he said being quoted out of context."

It's very seldom spoken about on the team, but you can sense an undercurrent. There are guys on the Lakers who are friendly, but relationships tend to be generally superficial, like those of a group of professionals going about their business. One reason, I think, is that players quickly realize the advantages of playing in Los Angeles and want to protect their interests. There are so many business and endorsement opportunities that you really can get into making it in LA. Also, the media are very active here and you can get a lot of exposure. The same thing is true of New York. I think this keeps us from becoming too close, because even though guys are your teammates, they are also a threat to your position as a member of the Lakers. There is no real togetherness as a team except on the court.

It's interesting that none of this necessarily has anything to do with the way a team plays. I don't know how it is in New York now, but from talking to a couple of Knicks in past years, I understand that they had the same sort of situation. They didn't associate much off the court, and in fact there were some guys who didn't particularly care for each other. But when you watched them play, it was beautiful. They passed the ball around and looked for the open man, and the guy who had the best shot took it. The play between the guards and the forwards was the way it should be. Everybody on the Knicks was involved in every aspect of the game. It seems as if they realized they had a job to do and overlooked personal conflicts. Maybe it was Red Holzman, their coach, or maybe it was the players, but they seemed to have decided they had a potential championship team and they got themselves together.

I found the Bullets to be a closer team than the Lakers. We got together a lot off the court, sometimes at a player's house and other times at a restaurant or bar. Maybe it was because there was nothing else to do in the city of Baltimore, whereas in Los Angeles there are a dozen things happening all the time. In Baltimore it seemed to be us against the world. In Los Angeles everybody fans out to his own section of the

91

city once the games or practices are over. Since nobody really wanted to be in the city of Baltimore, the Bullets weren't uptight about what was said about them. The attitude was, "We are all here together until we can get out." In Los Angeles it's more, "I'm here and I want to stay and the hell with anybody else."

I don't mean to say there wasn't animosity on the Bullets. In a way, guys got on each other more than they do on the Lakers. Once, at a meeting after we lost a game, Archie Clark asked Gene Shue who should get the ball and take a shot late in the game if the score was tied. What he wanted to hear was, "You, Archie," which, as a matter of fact, is what Gene should have said. Archie would definitely be the man in a spot like that. Gene didn't say anything, though, but Wes Unseld did. He said, "Archie, if you open your mouth one more time, I'm going to knock all your teeth in." Gene would run his hand across his forehead in situations like that and you could see him thinking, My God, what is going on? It got very heavy.

That could never happen on the Lakers. Nobody is going to tell Gail Goodrich to keep his mouth shut, and everybody has more respect for Bill Sharman than the Bullets did for Gene Shue. I think the animosity on the Bullets came about because we weren't winning. In the end, we genuinely liked each other more in Baltimore than we do in Los Angeles.

NOVEMBER 6

We were just beginning practice this morning when it became clear that something was going on. Bill Sharman walked quickly over to the wall of the gym, grabbed a chair, and carried it to the inbounds line at the middle of the court. Jack

Kent Cooke took a seat. A moment later Pete Newell walked in, and the three of them talked for a few minutes while we did calisthenics and ran up and down the floor. We were all giving each other funny looks as if to say, "What's happening here?" Except for those few minutes the first day of practice, Cooke hadn't been around at all, and his attendance at a routine drill was unique as far as anybody could remember. Did it mean a trade? I'm sure we were all thinking the same thing.

Finally, Bill and Pete left Cooke alone and he just sat there on the sideline, intently watching what was going on. First, he'd look toward the end of the floor where the starting five were working out. Then he'd look in the other direction where the reserves were. It made us all very edgy.

"God damn, I wish he'd get out of here," Bill Bridges whispered as we were taking shooting practice. "I can't hit a thing."

I took a shot from the key and it went in. "Hell, I'm hitting all my shots," I said. "Have him stay. I'm great under pressure." We tried not to laugh too noticeably.

Pretty soon Cooke called Pete over again, and in a second Pete called down to the other end of the floor, "Elmore, come here." Everything sort of stopped as they walked into a room off one end of the court. It was maybe 20 minutes before they came back.

After practice I walked out to the car with Elmore and asked him what it was all about.

"The same old shit, man," he said. "They asked me what was wrong with me and I told them my mind was on my religious commitment."

"What did Pete say to that?"

"Oh, you know, man. He talked about all the money I'm making and how it's my career and how pro basketball is really valuable to me."

"He's really right, you know."

"I don't agree, Stan. I'd rather be a serious and dedicated Jehovah's Witness than play professional basketball."

"Elmore, be a serious and dedicated Jehovah's Witness in the off-season. Do it all the time, as much as you want. And then in three or four years when you retire, go into it heavy."

"In three or four years," he said, "the world might not be here."

I didn't have an answer for that.

NOVEMBER 7

Bill Bridges was waiting for me when I came to practice today.

"Did you see Happy's little thing on TV last night?" he said.

"No," I said, wondering what he meant. "What?"

"He said the forwards are getting a bad rap," Bill said, "that the reason we're not scoring is the guards are selfish and won't give up the ball."

"No shit," I said.

So it was finally out in the open. Good. It's about time. But then I thought about how mad the front office would be. You don't say things like that on the Lakers. Especially when things aren't going well. And sure enough, Bill Sharman and Happy met for about 20 minutes before practice started. I was pretty sure they weren't talking about the best method of screening guys out away from the backboard in rebounding situations.

The locker room itself was pretty quiet, but you could tell there was only one subject on people's minds. Everybody is very nervous about the way things are going, and for Happy to say something like this now only brings our problems closer to the surface. It's like sticking your head out of the cellar during a hurricane. It's safer to just wait until it passes and hope you won't be blown away. Maybe if we were going better, there might have been some jokes about it. Of course, if we were going better, Happy might not have said anything.

Out on the floor I tried to be as inconspicuous as possible as I went over to Happy and gave him five. "Way to go," I said.

Happy smiled and said, "I think I'm right."

"So do I," I said. "But what do the people upstairs think?"

"Hell, they're furious. You know what Sharman just told me? He said he had to talk Newell and Cooke out of trading me. Shit. Do you think I can help some team?"

"I would imagine so." I laughed. "Anybody would love to have a strong rebounder."

"Yeah, it's all so ridiculous."

I thought about it during practice and I realized that Happy was really the only player who could have said what he did publicly. Next to Gail Goodrich, he's the most secure guy on the team. It was good that he spoke up, I thought, and I admire him for it.

NOVEMBER 8

The Knicks blew us out tonight 117–105, and it was pretty hard for me to keep my mind on the game. For one thing, they outscored us 34–15 in the first period, so it was all over early. And for another, I was thinking about something Bill Bridges had said.

"Something's up," he told me on the bench just before the start of the game. "We're getting another guard and you're going to get a lot more playing time."

"How do you know?" I asked him.

Bill just smiled as if to say, "Wait and see." I didn't have to wait long.

As we were walking down the long hallway to the dressing room after the game, Bill Sharman took Jim Price aside and waited until everybody else had gone ahead. In a minute Jim walked into the room and started going around shaking people's hands, saying good-by. It took a minute for it to sink in. He'd been traded. Soon it was all over the room that he was going to Milwaukee for Lucius Allen in a straight trade of guards.

Everybody on the team was stunned. Nobody seemed to believe it. The Lakers had always talked Jim up as the coming star of the backcourt, the next Jerry West. In spite of his inexperience, nobody had doubted his talent or potential. We all had thought he was secure.

Jim tried to play it cool but he was terribly upset. As he walked around shaking hands, he was swearing and saying, "Let me out of this mess." He kept repeating it as if it were a chant. I was sitting on a table, taking off my shoes, when I saw Jim point across the room at Happy Hairston's locker. Happy was in the shower.

"That motherfucker there is cancer," he said very quietly.

I thought to myself, How weird all this is. One day a forward is blasting the guards and the next day a guard is traded. I know that what Happy said couldn't have had anything to do with the trade—the Lakers and Bucks must have been discussing it for a while—but it looked funny to Jim, I guess.

Jim came by and shook my hand. "It was nice getting to know you and nice playing basketball with you," he said. "I guess I'll see you later."

"Yeah," I said, "I'll see you." I couldn't think of anything else to say.

Pretty soon the reporters came storming in through the door to try to find out what was happening, and they all crowded around Jim.

"Hey," Bill Bridges said, "why don't you give this guy a break? He feels awfully bad. It would be cruel to start asking him questions right now."

So they left him alone for a while and asked other people what they thought of the trade. After a few minutes the reporters started coming over to Jim one or two at a time, but he just shook their hands and said he'd see them later. I don't think he ever answered any questions.

Finally, the room cleared out, and without anybody really noticing it Jim had gone. I looked down at the mimeographed box score and saw that in his last game as a Laker Jim Price had led the team with 26 points.

NOVEMBER 9

I wish I had movies taken from above of the start of practice today. It must have looked like some weird dance sequence or mating ritual. Instead of the normal routine of random activity —some guys shooting, some running up and down the court, others doing stretching exercises—we were all out on the floor in pairs. Two guys were under each of the six baskets in the gym, shooting a ball and talking. Shooting and talking. Shooting and talking. Then all of a sudden, as if on cue, we would all switch around and there would be two players at each basket again. But it would be two different players. This went on until just about everybody on the team had talked to everybody else.

There was only one topic of conversation—the trade. There is the feeling that it is only the beginning, that something else is going to happen, and it makes most of us very nervous. A television broadcaster said last night that the Lakers are just one trade away from being a contender, and when you hear that kind of talk you start wondering who might be next.

"You don't have to worry," Bill Bridges said to me. "They're saving you and Kermit because you're the new generation. It's us old guys who have to sweat it."

"Well, how come the new generation never gets into the ball game then?" I said. We both laughed.

While we were doing calisthenics, Happy Hairston asked me what I thought of the trade. I said it was all right, something we had to try. "I think it was super," Happy said. "Just super."

After thinking about it overnight, I decided the trade was probably a calculated risk, one worth taking. Jim Price may turn out to be one of the great guards in the league, but right now we're losing. What difference does it make whether we lose with him or with Lucius Allen? If a different type of guard can help, it seems to me we've got to try it. There's certainly nothing to lose.

It's like a story a reporter told me recently about a conversation that Harry Dalton, the general manager of baseball's California Angels, had with Frank Robinson. Robinson was mad when he found out the Angels had put him on the trading block last season and he confronted Dalton, who'd been a good friend over the years.

"Frank," Dalton said, "I don't need to pay you $170,000 a year to finish last. I can finish last without you."

Anyway, Pete Newell was quoted in the paper as saying, "We need Allen's quickness and we need a man to handle the ball on the fast break." In other words, a playmaker, a guard who'd move the ball around.

I think another reason they made the deal is Brian Winters. Part of the Lakers' thinking had to be that Brian has shown a lot of promise as a rookie so they could afford to gamble he'd develop even more. Brian came over to the house after the game last night and Cheryl, Steve, and I needled him a little.

"It's all your fault Jimmy got traded," I said. "They'd never have made that move if you'd been playing poorly."

"Hey, don't blame it on me," he said. He didn't want to think about it.

Toward the end of practice Connie Hawkins and I were standing around shooting free throws. I was kidding him about having played center against the Knicks on Sunday—he'd scored 24 points and looked sharp even playing out of position —when we saw Bill Sharman and assistant coach John Barnhill take Elmore Smith aside. Again? I thought. They talked for a few minutes and then John and Bill left. I walked over and asked Elmore what was going on.

"They don't know what's happening, these people," he said.

"What's the deal?"

"They're not going to start me any more. They are going to sit me down and let me 'observe' for a while."

"What do you think about that?"

"It's their problem, not mine."

"Listen, why don't you come over to the house for lunch?" I said.

"No, I think I might just go to a show or something," he said, and he turned and walked away. I don't think I've ever seen him so depressed.

NOVEMBER 10

I was sitting on the bench a few minutes before the game tonight, watching the Warriors warm up, when all of a sudden it hit me. For a minute the situation reminded me of one of those questions on the intelligence tests they used to give us in high school—the kind that went, "Pick out the word on the following list that doesn't belong with all the others."

Here's the list: Al Attles, Joe Roberts, Rick Barry, Keith Wilkes, Clifford Ray, Butch Beard, Charlie Johnson, Steve Bracey, Derreck Dickey, Charles Dudley, George Johnson, Phil Smith. That's the entire coaching staff and playing roster of the Golden State Warriors as of early in the 1974–1975 basketball season. (Jeff Mullins is out with a broken bone in his hand.) The one name that doesn't belong? Rick Barry, of course. He's the only man on the team whose skin is white.

It's amazing when you think about it. In a year when professional baseball is overcome with self-congratulation because it finally has a black manager; in a year when professional football fans in two major cities are seriously debating whether a black man has enough guts to be a starting quarterback; in that same year a professional basketball team, almost without notice, takes the floor with both coaches and nine-tenths of its team black.

The NBA has come a long way from the days when it finally integrated a few token blacks. Now it has reached the point where the only *white* player on a team leading its division is a superstar forward who routinely scores 30 or more points a game. I wonder if any of the Warriors ever kid Barry by telling him everybody knows white players have to be much better than black ones, because if management has a choice between two players of equal ability it will go for the soul brother every time.

The Warriors are hardly unique, of course. A lot of teams have only a couple of white players, and there are black coaches at Detroit, Seattle, Portland, and Washington this season as well as Attles at Golden State. There are two black general managers in the league, and three days ago a black lawyer, Simon Gourdine, was named deputy commissioner of the NBA. He has a good shot at replacing Walter Kennedy as commissioner soon, I'm told. Overall, professional basketball must be 75 or 80 percent black.

Financially, this puts the white players in a strong position. We probably get better contracts than we might otherwise because management feels it really needs us. The best recent example of this is Bill Walton. He's a fine player, of course, but when Portland refers to him as a franchise maker, it isn't only his ability the club is talking about.

It's strictly a business consideration. The white fans still make up the biggest part of the crowds because they have the most money. And just as black fans probably got tired of seeing five white guys running around the floor for so many years, so a lot of white fans must get tired of watching all-black teams. Everybody needs somebody he can identify with, especially since the black isn't the invisible man any more because of the way race consciousness has come to the front in the last 10 or 15 years.

There are people who think the increasing number of black players in the sport is the single biggest financial problem facing basketball because of white-fan reaction. Even Bill Russell, a black, has expressed this viewpoint. If the league starts to stagger under the weight of what we're being paid and the corresponding rise in ticket prices, then the fact that the people with the most money (whites) won't want to pay to see the people with the most basketball ability (blacks) may make the problem worse. Recently I saw the results of a study that showed attendance at baseball games tends to drop off when a black pitcher is scheduled to start. It's all part of the same thing.

When you get away from thinking about race in financial terms, there are other kinds of considerations. For instance, being in the minority is an entirely new situation for almost all the white players, something none of us has ever been faced with before. Sometimes, I try to imagine what it must have been like to have been one of the first black players to integrate a sport—it must have been very strange and difficult. But our situation just isn't comparable at all. The racial hatred that was prevalent in those days simply isn't there. I can't conceive, for example, of black guys getting up a petition and refusing to play with whites the way some of the Brooklyn Dodgers did when Jackie Robinson broke baseball's color line. Sure, there is animosity between blacks and whites, and race is often a part of it, but mostly it's just the normal antagonisms that come up between teammates no matter what their color. In other words, it's trouble between players who happen to be black and those who happen to be white.

I don't deny that there are prejudiced people playing basketball—whites who don't like blacks, blacks who don't like whites—but it's something that's kept so far under the surface

101

that it doesn't seem to affect day-to-day relationships, either on the court or off. Even when Gus Johnson called white players on the Bullets "white honky motherfuckers," it never really shook anybody up that much. Nor did the fact that I found some racist implications in what Connie Hawkins had to say in *Foul* affect my friendship with him.

The way the coach handles things can go a long way toward determining the racial situation on a team. At Baltimore Gene Shue always seemed to be teetering on the brink of letting things get out of hand—though they never did—and he never seemed to know what to do about it. There were a couple of older black players, for instance, who wanted to play more than they should have—for their own good or for the team's. And if Gene took them out of the game when they didn't want to come out, sometimes you'd hear them say, out loud on the bench, "Gene Shue, fuck you." This just freaked him out, and instead of talking to them about it privately— telling them the reasons for his substitution policy—he'd just leave them in longer than he should have. Now, this meant that some of the younger players, like me, didn't get their time in. We developed our own answer to this, and pretty soon Gene would hear, "Gene Shue, what's wrong with you?"

Two of the guys who got into a lot of arguments in Baltimore were Jack Marin, who is white, and Wes Unseld, who is black. Marin, a law student, is one of the most intellectual guys in the league and quite conservative and outspoken on social issues. Unseld is a very intelligent guy who is proud of his heritage and also not afraid to speak his mind. They got into a lot of arguments on the black-white situation in America and lectured each other at great length. Often, it got very heavy, and in the end I think it reached the point where they really didn't care for each other very much. But it never ended in shouting and it never divided the team. The rest of us just observed from a distance without openly getting involved.

On the Lakers a few other factors come into play. Los Angeles has had a tradition of great black players and great white ones, and they have always respected each other as athletes even when they didn't care for each other as people.

In fact, whatever factions and cliques there were seemed to cut across racial lines. Today, when race comes up at all, it's usually humorously, which is the healthiest way for a team to handle it. Say the coach absent-mindedly puts three or four white guys out on the court against three or four black ones during a scrimmage. Somebody—and he could be white or black—might easily say, "Hey, coach, this doesn't look good. You don't want your white (or black) guys to be pushed into the ground, do you?" And everybody will laugh.

Kermit Washington, a giant of a man and a really good guy, and I were kidding around once and I asked him, "Hey, Kermit, how did they do it?"

"How'd they do what?" he said.

"How'd they get you off the Empire State Building and into a gym?"

Connie Hawkins was standing nearby and he started laughing like hell.

"What are you laughing at?" Kermit said. "Have you looked in the mirror lately?"

Often, one of the black players will refer to the whites as "you all." Naturally, we come back by calling them the same thing. This came up after the game tonight, which we lost by three points to the Warriors. Kermit and I were watching Happy Hairston quite a bit and kind of winked at each other during some of his antics. Whenever a foul was called on a Warrior, for instance, he would hold his hands up over his head and applaud, as if he were leading cheers. Or if he made a good pass or a basket, he'd pat a teammate on the ass or give him five on the way back to the other end of the court. Most players don't like to see this kind of thing because it seems so show-offy and I think it gets the other team mad and gives it a lift.

Anyway, we were still in the game at the end when Happy committed a silly foul on Keith Wilkes, who made the free throws that clinched the win for the Warriors. Kermit and I looked at each other and groaned.

Later, in the shower, Kermit said, "You know, I wish Happy were white so I could say that's why I hate him."

103

"But Kermit," I said, "he is *definitely* black."

"Yeah, I know. God damn it!" he said, and he gave me five.

"Yep," I said, "Happy is not our problem. He is *y'all's* problem."

NOVEMBER 11

Looking out the window this morning, I almost felt detached from myself for a moment, out of sync with my surroundings. As if by magic, the bikinis and the bicycles, which had gone into hibernation for the winter, were back. They had sprouted up again overnight and they dotted the beach as far as I could see. It was one of those incredibly beautiful days you get once in a while on the beach during the winter. The wind blows the sky clear and the temperature hits 90. During the summer you take a day like this for granted and wonder when the heat is going to break, but this late in the year it seems like a miracle.

I knew that in town they must be stifling and complaining about the smog, but out here you can really appreciate a day like this. Sometimes I try to explain living in Manhattan Beach to people, but it can be hard. Most people get so wrapped up in the details of their lives that they can't always relate to a different way of doing things. Even when it's foggy and cold and the beach is deserted, I love it. I like to be upstairs in the house where I can see the ocean. The sunsets are amazing sometimes. I can look out at one of the streets leading down to the beach and see people who have pulled their cars over just so they can watch the sun go down.

Living here is also very convenient as far as getting around is concerned. I'm close to the airport, close to the

Forum, close to the practice gym at Loyola, close to just about anywhere I want to go. But except for things revolving around basketball, the truth is I don't often leave here. Unless I go south to see some friends or my family, I seldom get on the freeway. Once in a while Cheryl and I will go to a show, but mostly I just like to hang around the house. I listen to music —we have enough stereo equipment upstairs and downstairs to supply a good-sized recording studio—maybe read a little or walk on the beach. When we're not on the road, all that's required of me is a few hours a day at practice or at the games. It can really be very nice. At the moment it would be even nicer if we were winning a few basketball games.

I've been thinking some more about the racial balance of the NBA and I've come to the conclusion that I actually get a sort of perverse satisfaction from being able to play what is becoming more and more a black game. If only 25 percent of the league is white now, then I'm different from most of the guys who are in the game. And since fewer and fewer white players can compete here, it makes me feel good to be one of the few. In a way, it helps to keep my competitive level high. I think this is why I got so completely blown out of my head last season when I heard the rumor that I wasn't putting out against black players. It was all part of putting me in that pigeonhole again, an extension of my clothes and my looks and so forth. The vibes I was getting were: freaky hair, mustache, rock musician for a brother, does his own thing—almost black himself, in a way. By looking at me like that, people could deal with me on terms that were comfortable to them. And never mind what total horseshit it all was. If they only knew . . .

I look back now on the racial situation that prevailed while we were in high school and I wonder how we ever got through it without the worst kind of trouble. We were on the verge so many times it amazes me that nobody got killed or seriously hurt. This was in the mid-1960s, at the height of the militant civil rights movement, and I can't help but think how dangerous it was that a bunch of immature high school kids, who had experienced almost nothing away from their familes and close friends, should have been on the front lines of the most significant social struggle of our times.

Morningside High in Inglewood was integrating then. Kids were being bused in from Watts, which wasn't far away, and a lot of blacks were moving into the area. I'd say Morningside was about 10 percent black the year I started, and it reached about 50 percent by the time I graduated. It would be wonderful to say that we all got along beautifully, that the races mixed freely and developed mutual respect as soon as they got a chance to know each other. But it wouldn't be true, no more than it is in south Boston today.

The most explosive times were when I was a senior. Once my sister Stephanie was brushing her hair in the girls' restroom in school when a group of black girls walked in and one of them pushed her away from the mirror. Having the Love temper, Stephanie ignored the odds and charged right in, slapping at the girl who'd pushed her and yelling, "You can't do that shit to me." A tough woman, my sister.

Luckily, nobody got hurt, but that afternoon about 15 black kids followed her home trying to scare her. Stephanie confronted me with it: I was the big bad senior basketball player and her older brother and what was I going to do about it? At the time, I was going with a girl whose father was a policeman, so my friends and I called him. For a while Stephanie was escorted home by a cop, and pretty soon there were squad cars hanging around outside the school.

The situation was no better during basketball games. For one thing, we didn't have any black players because the best ones stayed at their own schools, where I guess they were more comfortable and could concentrate on basketball without having to worry about racial problems. But the league we played in had several all-black schools and there were some very difficult times.

One problem was the way some of the coaches, teachers, and parents—adults who should have known better—played on our emotions. In high school—and college too, to a lesser extent—feelings are far more important than they are in professional ball, where skills and knowledge of the game are the key factors. We were always being exhorted to get sky high for the games, to get all hyped up and go out and win for dear old Morningside. It was only natural for us to take the next step and look at the opposition as niggers we had to beat to uphold the honor of the white race.

At the beginning of one season—I can't remember if I was a junior or a senior—we played Compton High, which was all black, and we won by two points. It was a tough physical game, and when it was over the Compton players returned to the locker room to find that somebody had stolen the beautiful blue school blazers they were all very proud of. There was almost a riot right then and there.

Compton went through the rest of the season unbeaten while we lost four or five games, and we met again in the California Interscholastic Federation district playoffs at Inglewood High, a neutral court. The Compton players were still steaming about the loss of their jackets and they really wanted to kill us. But we beat them again. What happened next was almost inevitable, I guess.

Our fans, practically all white, rushed onto the gym floor to congratulate us. Then the Compton stands, all black, emptied and pretty soon the whole court was one huge brawl. It was unbelievable. The fans and a lot of the players were fighting, and it was quite a while before the police and school officials could separate everybody. We had cops in the locker room, cops on the bus, and a police escort surrounding us all the way back to Morningside. The next day a lot of teachers and students showed up at school with broken glasses, puffy eyes, and cuts and bruises. It took a long time before the tension subsided. Personally, I had a lot of hate inside me for what had happened and I don't think I became friendly with a single black student all the time I was in high school.

Fortunately, it was different in college. At first, I associated mostly with athletes—there were quite a few black ones at Oregon—and when I got to know them on a one-to-one basis, it didn't take long to see that they were a lot like me. They were striving for the same athletic goals I was, working hard to become good ballplayers. But this was a gradual process, and some of my own attitudes didn't disappear overnight. At the end of my sophomore season, for instance, the Black Student Union at Oregon called a boycott. I don't remember the specific grievances it wanted to call attention to—though I don't think they had to do strictly with athletics—but boycotts were happening at a lot of colleges in the 1960s. Anyway, the blacks on the basketball team didn't play in the final two games of the season. They asked the white players to boycott too, but none of us did.

My attitude was that it was an individual thing, that the blacks should boycott if they wanted to but shouldn't try to drag other people into it. I was on a scholarship, I had a career to think about, and I liked the coach well enough not to want to do something like that to him. I said I sympathized with what the blacks were trying to accomplish—even this was quite a step for me—but I didn't want to get personally involved in it.

I think Steve Belko, our coach, handled the situation well. He told the black players to do what they felt they had to do and there would be no recriminations. The next season nearly all the black underclassmen who had taken part in the boycott were back on the team and nothing was said about it.

NOVEMBER 12

On the plane to Seattle today Connie Hawkins and John Barnhill tried to get up their usual poker game.

"Hey, Lucius," one of them called over to Lucius Allen, "do you play?"

He said no and everybody laughed. "That's it," somebody shouted. "Send him back." Jim Price had been a regular in airplane card games.

Lucius got off to a pretty cold start in his first game, the one against the Warriors on Sunday, shooting 4 for 14 from the floor and winding up with 14 points. He seemed kind of tight, as if he were pressing, trying too hard to do well. Actually, the trade is a homecoming for him. He was a great star on two national championship teams at UCLA, and before the game Sunday a couple of kids paraded through the stands carrying banners they had obviously worked on all day: "Los Angeles Lakers Welcome Lucius Allen" and "Welcome Home, Lucius." It was a nice tribute.

Some reporters were eager to make him into an instant star too, and one guy on TV didn't let Lucius' opening-night nerves and poor performance stop him. He said Gail Goodrich got 32 points against the Warriors because Lucius had done the playmaking and allowed Gail to get free to score. That sounds pretty good except for one thing: Gail was hot in the first quarter and Lucius didn't get in the game until the second.

Just as we were getting ready to practice, Pete Newell came into the arena. Although Pete makes some trips with us, it was unusual for him to be along for a quick one-game hop like this one. I asked Rich Levin of the *Herald-Examiner* what he was doing up here.

"I asked Pete that," Rich said, "and he said, 'Things are too hot in LA and I don't mean the weather.'"

It's kind of ominous because we still felt the pressure of Jack Kent Cooke showing up at practice, of Elmore Smith sitting out the entire game against the Warriors, and of Jim Price being traded. We were warming up when Pete called us over to the sidelines, sat us down in the stands, and told us why he had come. It was to deliver a little speech.

"We've got to start winning," he said. "If we don't, there's going to be some changes made. If any of you don't feel you can give us 110 percent, then we'll try to help you out, get you somewhere else."

Then he said, "And any complaints we have, let's air them to me or Bill. We don't want to read this shit in the paper." He wasn't looking at Happy Hairston when he said it, but we all knew it was directed at him. It was very quiet for a while.

109

Later, Rich told me that Pete isn't staying for the game with Seattle tomorrow. He's going to Portland to watch the Knicks play the Trail Blazers.

"You know what happened the last time Pete went out of town, don't you?" Rich said. "He came back with Lucius Allen."

NOVEMBER 13

So much for pep talks from the general manager. We lost a tough game to the SuperSonics tonight 108–103. Connie Hawkins and I watched it from the bench—that's two straight games I haven't played in—but Elmore Smith started his comeback. After holding him out for five straight quarters, Bill Sharman sent Elmore in for the second quarter and he seemed grateful for the opportunity. At one point Elmore scored on one of the wickedest dunks I've ever seen. His arm went into the basket all the way up to his elbow. He had ten rebounds and nine points in 20 minutes. I hope he's untracked now and will really get going.

The Lakers know their future at center is with Elmore. Zelmo Beaty is fine in certain situations, but he can't play for great lengths of time any more, and besides this is his last year. My locker is next to his and every once in a while, when he's taping his ankles, he says, "Well, only 76 more to go," or however many more games there are left. Bill Bridges says he's had it too. He likes to play well and it's hard on him knowing he's slowing down. He says it's really work for him now. Hard work.

The Sonics have gotten off to a surprisingly good start this season—they're second to the Warriors in the division. But whether or not they get to the playoffs, it's clear they'll be really good soon. They have Spencer Haywood, one of the finest forwards in the league, and five rookies on their roster who all seem to be getting a lot of playing time and developing well. It makes me kind of jealous.

Before the game I chatted with Archie Clark, who said he's very happy in Seattle, especially playing for Bill Russell. Archie's had a bad rap in the past—one season he had a long holdout with the Bullets in a fight over money—and he's gotten into disagreements with some of his teammates and coaches. But we've always gotten along well and I think his reputation as a bad guy isn't justified. Lots of times a guy is bad-mouthed because he's outspoken and says what he thinks instead of playing the humble anything-you-say-coach game. Anyway, Bill Russell was quoted recently as saying about Archie: "If this is trouble, this is the kind of trouble I need."

After the game Seattle forward John Hummer came by the hotel and had a few beers with Elmore, Brian Winters, and me. He couldn't say enough good things about Russell. He said the man can really coach, has everyone's respect, and has everybody working very hard for him. Russell thinks about the things ballplayers think about, John said, like how to get the kind of shot you need and how to stay involved in the game. He's doing a great job with Tom Burleson, the 7-4 rookie center from Maryland, who many people thought would be too slow and awkward to be any good in the pros. Burleson is only 22—and he's an immature 22 instead of an experienced, polished one like Bill Walton is or like Kareem Abdul-Jabbar was—but he's aggressive and works hard and isn't afraid to dive on the floor. With Russell to teach him, he'll be a dynamic center in a few years.

I enjoyed talking to John. We'd met briefly before through some mutual friends on the East Coast, but we'd never really been able to sit down and rap. That's one of the things I'm really sorry about. There are some interesting people in the NBA, but with everybody on the go you seldom have a chance to put your feet up and talk with someone on another team. That means your only real relationship a lot of times is a competitive one. And it's amazing how much your feelings about an opponent *off* the court are influenced by your relationship with him *on* the court.

For instance, I am told that Jerry Sloan of Chicago is one of the nicest guys in the world when he isn't playing basketball. But on the floor he is just a killer. He beats up on everybody without regard to race, creed, height, or weight. I can't imagine anyone on any team except the Bulls being friendly with him.

Or there is the relationship I have had with Sidney Wicks of Portland over the years. We both grew up in Los Angeles and played against each other in pickup games when we were in high school. But we never really got to know each other. Sidney went to UCLA, which played Oregon twice a year, and those were the only times I saw him. He was extremely competitive and we had some real battles on the court and never could relate to each other when the game was over.

I remember in 1970—when UCLA won the NCAA title— they lost only two games, one to Southern California and one to us, by 13 points, in Eugene. After the game there was a party near where I lived, and all the UCLA players came. We tried to be friendly, but they were freaked out because they had lost and had very little to say. I tried to talk to Sidney about LA and some of the things we had in common, but he acted like I didn't exist. After a while most of us just figured, well, those are the snobbish UCLA players for you, and we ignored them. Since then, as Sidney and I have been in the NBA for a while, we've become more friendly. Maybe we've both learned there's more to life than what goes on inside the lines around the court.

I think a lot of us often get so involved in our own little part of the game that we lose sight of anything out there beyond the NBA. And it's a mistake, really, because we're losing our monopoly on it even if it is an American game.

My one experience with basketball outside of the United States happened this past August, before the season started, when a bunch of NBA and ABA players in the Los Angeles summer pro league were invited to play some exhibition games in Japan. They only paid expenses, but I jumped at the chance because I'd always wanted to go there. Besides, they paid Cheryl's way too.

We played seven games in various parts of the country, and they were very well attended. The Japanese were curious about our playing style, and after a while we saw that what they really liked were the spectacular plays: dunk shots, long jumpers, blocked shots, and so on. The pickup games we saw with Japanese players were very mechanical, without much real individual skill, so this was all pretty new to them. Soon we were all trying to outdo each other with stuff shots, through-the-leg dribbles, behind-the-back passes, and all the Globetrotter moves we knew. Our coaches back home would have screamed if they had seen us doing these things, but we had a lot of fun.

The Japanese were so anxious to please, so eager to make us feel at home, that they translated everything they could into English. In Tokyo we played in the beautiful arena they built for the 1964 Olympics, and as we were going down the hall to find our dressing room, we all started laughing. The signs on the doors said "Rocker Room No. 1" and "Rocker Room No. 2." Then, when they introduced us to the fans, they had all kinds of problems. I was Stan Rove of the Ros Angeres Rakers, which was pretty straightforward as far as that went, but both Nate Hawthorne and Harthorne Wingo were also with us, and the announcers just butchered the hell out of those names. After a while Nate was saying to anybody who would listen, "Do you know who I am?"

The remarkable thing about basketball in Japan is that even though a lot of people are playing it, you don't see many hoops around. The cities are so crowded that a lot of the recreation areas are on rooftops.You'd find a big building, maybe an apartment complex, and way up on the top would be a basketball hoop and a baseball diamond. Completely caged in, so they wouldn't lose the ball.

One of the places we played was Sapporo, on the northern Japanese island of Hokkaido. Cheryl and I got away for a day and took a cab up to the giant ski lift they built for the 1972

113

winter Olympics. We had the directions written down for the cab driver—that's the way you get around by cab in Japan—and he drove us through the city and up to the ski lift. We had to take a tram to get to the top and we bought the cab driver a ticket because we didn't want to lose him; he had to get us back. He didn't know what to make of the whole thing at first, but when we finally got through to him with gestures what we wanted him to do, he smiled and bowed and got in the tram with us.

I took some pictures on the way up, and when we climbed out of the tram at the top of the lift a mob of kids came running over to us, waving and chattering. Many of them were wearing American baseball caps and we couldn't figure out what was going on. Finally we realized that anybody who is 6-9 and blond and suddenly drops into their midst is bound to create a little interest. There must have been 50 kids altogether, and they were there on some kind of school outing. Pretty soon they were running in circles around us. One climbed on top of another and they laughed like hell because now the two of them were as tall as I was. Then some of them put their feet and their hands alongside mine to measure the difference. One kid grabbed my camera bag and followed us around the whole time we were up there. If you let a kid have your bag outside the Forum, I thought, that would probably be the last you'd see of it. But somehow I knew the last thing this kid wanted to do was rip off my bag. He was a hero to his friends just by carrying it for me.

After a while it seemed as if they were all touching me, rubbing the hair on my arm, which the Japanese don't have, and laughing. Cheryl became an instant celebrity too. They were touching her hair and she was signing autographs. They took pictures of us and we took pictures of them; I think we all ended up with pictures of people taking pictures. We tried to talk to them, tell them I played basketball, but it didn't seem to matter that we couldn't understand each other. We were having a great time.

Finally, we got back in the tram and started back, waving to them as we went slowly down the mountain while they waved at us from the top. I had a lot of fun in Japan and enjoyed playing basketball there, but I think fooling around with those kids on the top of that mountain was the nicest experience of the whole trip.

NOVEMBER 15

Lynn Shackelford was nervous. It was 7:00 A.M. yesterday—time for the bus to leave for the Seattle airport and the trip home—and Connie Hawkins was missing. Lynn asked Frank O'Neill to ask Bill Sharman whether we should leave without the Hawk. "You ask him," Frank said. Lynn does the color commentary on the radio and TV broadcasts—he's become a master at getting a few words in during the five-second intervals Chick Hearn gives him—and is also the Lakers' traveling secretary.

"No, you ask him," Lynn said, obviously not enjoying the situation at all.

So Frank called out, "Bill, Hawk's not here. We called his room several times and there's no answer and it's seven o'clock."

"We'll wait a few more minutes," Bill said.

"Are you happy now?" Frank said to Lynn, and we all snickered a little.

After five more minutes and another call to Connie's room, the bus left without him and he missed the plane. It's no big deal really, but when we got home last night it was all over television along with an interview with the Hawk that had been filmed a couple of days earlier. He said this was the first year he hadn't been a regular starter and he didn't like it, which is a ballsy thing to say in public. Later in the interview

115

he backed off a little and said he'd do whatever Bill wanted him to, but the words still had a bite to them.

The Hawk and I have talked about it over the last few days and he said he's getting a taste of what it's like to come off the bench. "I can relate to what you've been doing the last couple of years," he said. "Man, I can't believe how hard it is. What's the most minutes you've ever played in one game?"

"I think it's something like 28 minutes," I said. "I haven't played much because of guys like you—you asshole." And we both laughed.

Rich Levin wrote about Connie's missing the bus in the *Herald-Examiner,* and he had it in better perspective than the television reports; he didn't make it sound like it was some big crisis. Rich is the only reporter who travels with us all the time so he has by far the best feel for what's important and what isn't. Perhaps, if the *Times* sent a reporter with us on the road all the time, Rich would have played the story up bigger for fear that the opposition paper might be hitting it hard and he'd look like he wasn't on top of things.

It's strange, really, that Rich's paper is the only one that has a reporter with us all the time. The *Times* is a much more widely read paper than the *Herald-Examiner,* far more influential and wealthy, but for some reason it almost never covers us on the road. Mal Florence, who writes most of the home games for the *Times* and who we all like because he has that athlete's sense of humor (heavy on the needle), tells a wonderful story about this.

When the Lakers won the NBA title and went on that 33-game win streak three years ago, it was really a big story with a lot of national attention. But not until they broke the old record for consecutive wins—20 by Milwaukee—did the *Times* cover them on the road. And as they kept winning and winning, Mal stayed with them.

The streak came to an end in a nationally televised game in Milwaukee, but the Lakers had a couple of games left on the road trip and interest was still very high. Would the team keep on losing now? Would it start winning again? Papers all over the country were still playing it at the top of the sports page.

The Lakers stayed over in Milwaukee before going on to

116

their next game in Detroit, and Bill Sharman and a few of the players were standing around in the hotel lobby when Mal came out of the elevator with his suitcase and typewriter and headed for the door.

"Mal," Bill called out, "where are you going?"

"Sorry, Bill," Mal said, "I don't cover losers." And he walked out the door, got a cab for the airport, and went home.

NOVEMBER 16

Bill Walton seems to be running into a little cultural shock. Just about everybody does when they finally realize they're out of college and things are a little different in the NBA. Walton has been out of Portland's lineup for a couple of days with a dislocated finger, and the team is hassling him to get back in there.

"Damn, they want me to play," he said before the game in Portland tonight. "I tried and it took me three days to get my hand so I could hold it below my waist."

Walton has it tougher than most rookies coming into the league. He's supposed to take the Trail Blazers into the playoffs immediately (they were 27 and 55 last season, last in the division) the way Kareem Abdul-Jabbar did when he first went from UCLA to Milwaukee. But it hasn't happened. Portland is playing around .500 and only in third place. Even though Walton has had some outstanding games, he just hasn't been as dominating as Abdul-Jabbar. Is anybody? For one thing, Walton is 7-0 and Kareem is easily 7-4. He just towers over even the biggest guys in the league. And for another, Walton still lacks pro experience. It'll take him a few times around the league to get adjusted.

There's just so much to get used to. Playing 48-minute

games 82 times a year instead of 40-minute games 30 times a year is one of the things you have to adjust to coming out of college into the NBA. But there are other things that can be even more disconcerting. In college the refs call fouls almost any time there is significant physical contact. But in the pro game much more body contact is allowed. It seems somebody is always grabbing you, and it's very hard to get used to playing with somebody's hand on your ass all the time. Some of the strong forwards in the league can guide you just about wherever they want. After a while I learned to move around a lot, trying to run the defender into screens and keep him a few feet away so he couldn't grab me. Dealing with the much rougher style of play in the NBA can be a tough adjustment.

The ironic thing is that I had the reputation for being a pretty rough player in college. *Sports Illustrated* said I was the most misnamed player of the year because I was kicking and spitting all the time. Which is an exaggeration. I never spit at anybody. I think my reputation got started my first year when Oregon's freshmen were playing Oregon State's. We had lost only one game, and their big center, a guy named Pete Parsons, was constantly on my back, going over the top of me. Oregon–Oregon State games were generally pretty rough to begin with—even when it was only the freshmen—and the referees were relatively lenient; they liked to let us play without calling a lot of fouls.

In the second half, when things were really getting out of hand, Parsons and I were battling for a rebound and I put an elbow in his chest. He stumbled and fell flat on his back. I got the ball and threw it out to one of my teammates and started going up the court. Parsons was lying in my path, and without even thinking about it I just stepped on his chest and kept on going. It was an unusual thing to do, but he had been on me all night and there he was right in front of me. As soon as I stepped on him, I couldn't believe what I'd done. You can get that way in a game sometimes. There were a lot of Oregon State fans there and they just went berserk. Some of them wanted to come out of the stands and get me and they didn't let up on me the rest of the game.

I'm afraid I'm not quite that aggressive any more. It's one thing to shove guys around in college, but it's a completely different story in the NBA. I'm not going to go knocking Wes Unseld around. He'd kill me.

One thing is in Walton's favor, though. The fans in Portland seem to have taken to him and accepted him for what he is. He wears his hair long and keeps it out of his eyes with an Indian-style headband, but nobody seems to get on him for it. I don't know whether the times have changed or the people in Portland are just more tolerant, but I don't hear the redneck kinds of things I sometimes did in Baltimore. I had a full beard there for a while and every so often somebody in the stands would yell, "Hey, Love, shave your beard, you freak!"

On the Lakers the word has gotten around that Jack Kent Cooke doesn't like beards, so only Connie Hawkins wears one. The Hawk doesn't care what anybody thinks. But the rest of us do, I guess, and the general feeling is why do something that will get them upset? Gail Goodrich, for instance, sometimes grows a beard in the off-season, and once a picture of him wearing it appeared in a magazine. Last season somebody asked him, "How come you don't grow one now?"

"Do you think the man upstairs would like it?" he said. Everybody knew what he meant. Pat Riley had a beard last season, but this year it's gone. I think he just realized it was smarter not to have one.

At any rate, during the game tonight, Walton just sat on the bench wearing a lumberjack shirt and a red bandanna in his long hair, looking like a guy who'd come down out of the mountains to see the game.

The bus ride back to the hotel tonight was a quiet one. The Trail Blazers, even without Walton, beat the crap out of us 112–99. It was our fifth loss in our last six games and a terribly weak performance. I hated watching it. Which was all I did. It's the fourth straight game I haven't played in.

When I got off the bus at the hotel, Bill Sharman was about 15 or 20 feet in front of me; he looked back and waited for me to catch up to him.

"Can I speak to you for a minute?" he asked.

"Sure," I said, and we walked into the lobby and sat down on a couch.

"I want you to know I appreciate your good attitude," he said. "It makes it a lot easier on me."

Funny, I thought. My attitude *has* been better. I haven't been down as much lately. Maybe I figured my time would come. And maybe this was it.

"I'm unhappy with the play of the forwards," Bill said, "and I want you to work all next week with coach Barnhill and coach Creger. Work out hard and get in extra running because I'm going to be using you. There's no question about your offensive ability; your rebounding is adequate and so is your passing. But you've got to work hard and really try to learn the defense."

"All right," I said, trying not to show my excitement, "I'll try."

"I know I've been giving Hawkins and Bridges prolonged shots at working into the rotation," he said. "I feel I owe it to them because Hawkins made the All-Star team one year and Bridges made the All-League team. But I'm just not happy with the way they're playing."

We talked for about 15 minutes, or rather Bill did. I just listened mostly and tried to absorb what he was telling me. He indicated that he didn't necessarily mean I'd play tomorrow against Chicago in the Forum, and we don't have another game for five days. That seems to be the one he's pointing toward. Then Bill called both Barnhill and Creger over and told them to work with me on defense next week, to point their energies toward me for a while.

Finally, our meeting broke up and I went to my room. I had a little trouble falling asleep.

NOVEMBER 17

On the plane ride home today I sat down across the aisle from Happy Hairston.

"Stanley," he said with his widest grin, "I hear we got some good news last night."

Everybody knew about my meeting with Bill Sharman by then. Something like that doesn't stay quiet for very long.

"Yeah, I got some good news," I said.

"Well, listen," Happy said, "get to practice early, run hard, work hard, just run and shoot and play that defense as hard as you can."

Thanks, Happy, I thought to myself as he continued his pep talk. I couldn't really be upset with him, though. I was thinking nice thoughts about the whole world. I was finally going to get my chance. After a while I even started thinking how nice it was of Happy to be so helpful.

The game tonight was unbelievable. I'm still not sure how it happened. Chicago beat us 96–76. It was the fewest points the Lakers have scored in a regular-season game since they moved here from Minneapolis 14 years ago. In the first quarter we scored 14 points. In the first *half* we scored 32. We fell into last place in the Pacific Division, five and a half games behind the Warriors. And we heard the worst booing I've ever experienced at the Forum.

I'm almost ashamed to mention that I got in for the first time in five games, playing the last 15 minutes and scoring 13 points. Now there's a stat. The Lakers get their lowest point total in 1,066 games and I get my highest total of the season. At least it's a running start into Friday.

Bill Sharman kept the dressing room door closed for 33 minutes, which somebody said is the unofficial record. The interesting thing was that it was one of our best team meetings of the season. Nobody tried to put the blame on anybody else, which happens sometimes. You might get a guy saying the forwards aren't hustling or the guards aren't passing and then somebody else will speak up and say, "I resent that shit." Usually, though, if something like this happens a couple of other guys will jump right in and say, "Hey, why are you talking like that? Let's discuss this like human beings and professionals." And the guy who started it will most often apologize.

But tonight it was all very constructive. Just about everybody had something to say about what was wrong and a lot of it made sense. I said I thought we weren't being aggressive enough at the start of the game, that we didn't jump right out on them with our hands and push and shove and hold and grab the way the other teams do. My feeling is you can't let the other team start out aggressively and then, in the second quarter, say to yourself, "Hey, they're playing a little rough tonight; let's do the same thing," because the refs will see you playing harder all of a sudden and call fouls on you. But if you establish a rugged approach at the start of the game, you have a better chance of getting away with it.

Jerry Sloan of the Bulls, who's a noted hatchet man, beat us up like mad tonight, but he got away with it because that's just his normal style of play. In fact, somebody pointed out that the Bulls had only one foul called on them in the whole second quarter, which is ridiculous.

I also think that we might be making too much of a thing out of playing good defense. When you score only 76 points in a game, you ought to think more about the offense. Anyway, it was a good meeting after having played so badly. Lucius Allen and I discussed it a little in the shower afterward. Except for 24 points in our win over Philadelphia two nights ago, Lucius has been having trouble getting started. Tonight he had only eight points, but considering the way we played as a team I don't think anybody can possibly hold the loss against him.

"What would Costello be doing at this point?" I asked him.

"Oh, man," he said, "he'd be yelling and screaming and threatening us with trades."

He was obviously impressed that Bill keeps things on a level of what we can do to improve rather than just yelling at people.

NOVEMBER 18

I feel like I have a telephone receiver growing out of my ear. It seems as if I've spent all day talking to people. My teammates are starting to call me Dr. Love. Everybody's consulting me on what's wrong with us. I only wish I had the answer. But we certainly had a lot to talk about today.

First, there was what Bill Sharman told the press after the game last night. He said he was going to meet with Jack Kent Cooke to discuss possible trades and future lineup changes. Well, you can't blame him for looking around at possible trades, though Bill himself said, "This time of year, who is going to trade a quality player?" And we already know about at least one lineup change that's coming. The business about meeting with Cooke, however, sounded a little ominous. We all wondered what it meant.

But even more interesting is some of the stuff Chick Hearn said on the radio last night. A couple of my friends called and said that just before the second half he got very upset. Apparently, it went like this:

"Jack Kent Cooke is coming back from his ranch in Bakersfield and I know he's not happy with the way things are going and I know I can speak for him when I say he'll be making the moves that have to be made. The Lakers have never failed to make the playoffs since they came to Los Angeles and this organization is dedicated to producing a winner for the basketball fans of the southland."

Chick quite naturally gets somewhat upset when things aren't going well, but he's never gotten into it that heavily, making threats and promises and almost begging the fans not to stop buying tickets to the games.

Another topic of conversation was the fact that the first NBA coach of the season was fired: Scotty Robertson of New Orleans. He came right out of a college in Louisiana and stepped in with an expansion team, so nobody expected the Jazz to make the playoffs. But when a team loses 14 of its first 15 games, something is bound to happen. Still, a firing is something everybody in the league can relate to. It brings your mortality close to home, especially when you're doing a lot of losing yourself.

During the day Kermit Washington checked in and said Bill Bridges had told him he was through, that he was quitting this week. Bill told him he'd just had enough. I'm not sure I believe it. Bill is a good man, but he's like all the rest of us: he talks kind of crazy every once in a while and he might just be down. We'll have to wait and see. Practice should be pretty interesting tomorrow.

Then, on the six o'clock news, one of the sportscasters said, "Here's what's wrong with the Lakers." And up on the screen appeared a picture of Elmore Smith. I immediately called Elmore and asked him if he'd seen it. He had.

"You know the big man always has to take the blame," I said. "Don't worry about it. Just go out there and do the best you can. Don't let that shit bother you. You listen to enough of it and it can rot your mind." I don't know if it helped. Elmore really sounded bugged.

But the biggest blow of the whole day came later in the evening when Pat Riley called. We were talking about December 1, which is the last day you have to be on the roster in order to get your whole salary. Then Pat dropped his bomb.

"They let Frank go," he said.

124

"WHAT?!"

"Yeah, they hired a guy named Del Tanner, a trainer at Dana Point High School."

That was quite a surprise to me. Del Tanner was the trainer at Morningside High when I was there. Frank O'Neill is the dean of NBA trainers. He's been with the Lakers since they came to Los Angeles in 1960. There has never been even the slightest hint that he might be in trouble. According to Pat, a couple of things did him in. First, he's been trying to get a raise for a couple of years now. He can't be making much money.

Another thing is that Elmore has been complaining about the way Frank has been taping his bad ankle. Elmore's discouraged that it hasn't been getting any better and I guess he blames Frank for it. He went to somebody in the front office and said Frank was fucking up his ankle. That was the last straw, I guess. They just threw him out on the street without any warning. It was really a cold move.

I called Frank to tell him how sorry I was. He was really down. He called Elmore all kinds of names and said how stupid he was. It wasn't *his* fault that his ankle didn't get any better, Frank said. He'd told him to go to the doctor about it and to take whirlpool baths, and he'd tried different ways of taping it. What else could he do? He said Bill Sharman and John Barnhill asked Cooke not to cut him loose, to at least wait until the end of the season. But Cooke had made up his mind and fired him. They're supposed to put out a cover story that Frank is quitting to go into private business.

I was really low when I hung up. Having a new trainer around can only create more tension. Guys won't want to talk around him for a while until they see what he's like. We all got along with Frank and trusted him. We knew he would never carry tales to the front office about what went on in the locker room. I know that Del will be all right—he's a good man—but it's only natural for players to be a little distrustful of a new guy. At least for a while.

Jeez, what a day this has been.

NOVEMBER 21

Love has averaged only six points a game, but he's played only 13.3 minutes a game. That works out to an average of 27.4 points for every 48 minutes of playing time. Moreover, he has been the Lakers' most accurate shooter, at 54 percent.

Thanks, Mal Florence, I needed that. An average of 27.4 points a game! Are you kidding me? What an awful thing to put in the paper. It's misleading for one thing. So much of the time I've played has been when the game was decided, when the other team's reserves were in and the competitive edge was lost. I hope nobody's expecting anything like that.

Elmore Smith and I have been the center of attention since Bill Sharman announced to the press two days ago that we would start against Houston tomorrow. I wish there were a way to just slide into it unnoticed, but there isn't. Dick White, our publicity man, has been giving me messages to call this reporter and that reporter, but I don't really want to do it.

"They're nice guys, Dick," I said, "but they haven't talked to me all year. Why would they want to talk to me now?"

"Well, they've been expecting Love in the lineup."

"Yeah," I said. *"Bob* Love." We both laughed.

During practice today a TV crew showed up. It was from the same channel that ripped Elmore the other day, though a different reporter was there. He wanted to interview both of us, but Elmore wouldn't do it. He's still mad at what they said about him and I don't really blame him. I didn't want to go on either, but I finally did.

There's so much to think about. Rudy Tomjanovich, for instance, the Houston forward I'll be guarding tomorrow. He's a big, rugged guy who rebounds well and can shoot from the outside. He's having a fine year, averaging 21 points a game, and he's always done well against the Lakers. Last season he had 28.5 points a game against us.

Then there's the realization that I have so much to learn about fitting in, knowing what everybody on the court will do at any given time. A guy like Lucius Allen, for example, likes to pop out behind a forward on a screen, and you've got to know how long he usually stays out there and whether he cuts back and pops out again or continues to go around you to get to the other side. On defense you have to communicate with everybody, shout "Pick left" or "Pick right," and then try to get around a guy before he can set a good screen on you. It's difficult for the other guys to work with somebody who they haven't really played with for any length of time all season. Obviously, it's going to take a little while. I only hope we can win this weekend because it will give me a little longer to settle down. Bill said he wants to give me a real shot at starting. I hope that means a couple of weeks, not just one or two games. But it all depends on whether we win or not. If we don't, I know he'll change things again. I'm not kidding myself. I know it's a desperation move on his part. We're 5 and 9, in the cellar and falling fast. All I can do is try my best and hope things work out.

I've had a couple of good talks with Bill and he said he wants me to do five things, in this order: (1) play good defense; (2) rebound; (3) score; (4) pass well so we can cut down on turnovers (we've been averaging 25 a game); and (5) run. Scoring, which is my strong point, is pretty far down the list considering that the team had only 76 points in its last game, but Bill has a thing about defense. That's what he wants me to concentrate on the most.

Under the circumstances, I feel pretty good. A little nervous maybe, but that's OK. This will be the first time I've ever started as a Laker. In fact, it's really the first time I've started a professional game that meant anything. During my second season in Baltimore I started a few times after we had made the playoffs and Gene Shue wanted to give the regulars a rest. I remember we were playing Cleveland, and Steve Patterson, a good friend and underrated ballplayer, came over to my place the day of the game. I had no idea I'd be starting and we ate a late steak dinner. When Gene told me an hour before the game that I was starting, I was sitting there with a full stomach, thinking, Oh, my God! It worked out all right, though. I played over half the game and scored 28 points, my career high.

I've started a crash program with my back exercises this week too. Dr. Kerlan would be proud of me. Part of the reason for it is that my back has started to hurt again lately. I wonder if I'm wacko or something. Here I'm getting my chance and my back starts to hurt. Anyway, I'm doing my pelvic tilt, my knees-to-chest back stretch, my partial situps, my toe-touching, and all the other exercises Dr. Kerlan has written out on two sheets of paper for me.

Incidental bits of intelligence:

Jack Kent Cooke was at practice *again* today. I could live without that. It's almost like he's saying, "You guys better straighten this shit out or I'm going to trade you, *all* of you."

Jim Price scored 43 points for Milwaukee two nights ago. Looks like that might have been the proverbial trade that helps both teams.

NOVEMBER 22

I have some good news and some bad news. The good news is we won tonight, beating Houston 89–83. The Rockets had won four straight, and 9 of 11 going into the game, and we'd lost 6 of 7 so it was a good win.

The bad news is I was awful. No, wait. I take that back. I was half awful. I did all right on defense. Rudy Tomjanovich only got a few baskets off me and I had nine rebounds and a blocked shot. Also, I think I moved around reasonably well on offense. What was awful was my shooting. My *shooting*. The strongest part of my game. The one thing I don't have to worry about. I was 2 for 12. Four points. How embarrassing.

I was just so tight going in. It seemed like I had 80 people telling me what to do. Everybody on the team tried to help me out with advice. Bill Bridges told me how to play guys defensively. Happy Hairston told me to shoot, not to worry about rebounds. Elmore Smith told me to turn the man I was guarding into him on defense, not to worry about him myself. It all ended up being more harmful than helpful, I think.

Fortunately, the game started out almost as slowly as I did. Both teams sort of stood around waiting for something to happen. I took a couple of early shots that were good opportunities, but it seemed like I was too strong, putting the ball up too hard. I came out of the game toward the end of the first period but was back in early in the second just in time to really screw up a play. Kermit Washington took a good rebound off the defensive board and lobbed a beautiful pass to me down at the other end for what should have been an easy layup. And I fumbled the ball out of bounds.

Houston put together a pretty decent second period and led by seven points at the half. But we caught up in the third period and finally I started doing something offensively. Halfway through the quarter I got open about 18 feet from the basket and took a shot. It felt just right as it left my hand and I remember thinking, If this one doesn't go in, I'm getting out of here. But it was good, my first basket after missing seven straight shots. A minute or two later Gail Goodrich was bringing the ball down the court when I saw an open path through the key and moved toward the basket. Gail lobbed the ball to me up high and I put in a stuff shot and got fouled. Even missing the free throw couldn't take away the enjoyment of the moment. That basket brought us within a point, and a little while later Happy tied the game with a free throw and soon we went ahead to stay.

Bill Sharman used a lot of strange lineups in the game. At one point Kermit was at center, Bill Bridges and I were at forward, and Pat Riley and Lucius Allen were in the backcourt. He's really experimenting. In a way, we were lucky to win because we shot only 38.9 percent as a team from the floor. But Houston was worse, 36 percent, and scored only 33 points in the second half.

"We certainly didn't win that game on offense," Bill said later in the locker room. He didn't say anything to me, but a reporter said he'd told the press I'd seemed a little tight, but that he'd been pleased with my defense and rebounding. He'd said Tomjanovich got only three or four shots off me.

It's a start.

NOVEMBER 24

Very early in the game against Washington tonight Wes Unseld went up for a shot and I blocked it cleanly from behind. The referee called a foul.

What is this? I thought and then shrugged it off, which is the only way to handle a bad call. You get your share and you just have to try to forget them and go on and play the game.

A minute or so later I made a move to set a screen and bumped into a guy. Another foul, legitimate this time. Pretty soon I set another screen, cleanly, and one of the Bullets stepped into *me*. Only that's not what the referee called. We'd played four minutes and I had three fouls. I spent the rest of the half on the bench wondering why these things happen to me and thinking about referees.

They have differing abilities, just like anyone else, I guess. In the NBA I would say the range is from good to very bad. The best ones—refs like Richie Powers, Mendy Rudolph, and Darell Garretson—seem to be the ones who are the hardest to intimidate. When you have a Kareem Abdul-Jabbar yelling down at you, you can get rattled, and some refs tend to let the more dominating guys get away with things rather than calling what they see.

Another problem is that some referees play reputation rather than the game on the floor. In a lot of cases an established veteran might get the benefit of the doubt. Once in New York I was guarding Dave DeBusschere when he drove toward the baseline, lost his footing, and fell. Immediately, the referee blew his whistle and pointed at me. I hadn't touched him, but since it was DeBusschere, one of the great forwards

131

in the league, he couldn't have just fallen, the ref seemed to assume. I must have fouled him.

Then there are the guys whose style of play is rough. Jerry Sloan of Chicago should foul out in the first quarter of almost every game he plays, that's how much he beats up on people. The refs must say to themselves, "Well, that's not too bad for Sloan," or they'd be whistling him down all the time. The same is true for guys like Bill Bridges and, when he was playing, Gus Johnson. Their method of defense is very close to fouling because they hold so much. I think they get away with it more than a younger player because they've been around so long.

The thing you hope for in referees is consistency. A lot of times you find they just aren't calling plays the same way during games and that can make things very difficult. Most teams start out kind of feeling their way around with the officials, trying to see what they're calling that night. Are there a lot of offensive fouls? Are they enforcing the three-second rule strictly? Are they calling things closely in general? At halftime Bill Sharman will bring it up with us, remind us how the calls are going, and tell us to be careful not to commit the kind of fouls the refs seem to be looking for. Of course, the refs can change their calls in the second half, but you have to hope you're going to get them on a consistent night.

All coaches get on referees to some extent—I don't think there's any way to avoid it considering how far the officiating goes toward determining who wins the games—but sometimes it really gets out of hand. One night in Baltimore Manny Sokol really seemed to have it in for us. It appeared that he was going out of his way to screw us. And Gene Shue was just climbing the walls. At one point, when Sokol made a terrible call—the kind where the whole arena starts booing—Shue put his hands over his face and screamed, as loud as he could, "Manny Sokol, I hate your fucking guts!"

I have a tendency to react badly to questionable calls. I find it difficult not to get upset, especially when the calls are just so poor that you want to explode. What I try to think of is something a coach—I forget who it was—once said: You've got to play the call like any other part of the game, a bad bounce or a missed free throw or anything else that shouldn't happen but does. You get called for a foul, the other guy gets a free throw, and you take it from there. Something else to remember is that the referees hate looking bad as much as anybody else. They're in a situation where half the people in the game are going to hate them whatever they do and they don't like being shown up. I had a long talk with Darell Garretson once on a plane and he told me not to react to calls to the extent where it embarrasses the officials, which is good advice. Of course, it's a lot easier to be rational about this when you're sitting around talking than when you're out on the court fighting for a job and someone sees to it that you get only 11 minutes of playing time. That is not what I had in mind at all tonight, needless to say. Neither is getting beaten by Washington by three points. There goes our one-game win streak.

NOVEMBER 25

Here it is a month into the season and we're just now making our first trip away from the West Coast. Sometimes it seems as if the schedule is made up by Santa Claus and other times by Attila the Hun. We had several stretches of five days off at home early in the season where all we could do was practice until we were sick of it. But now we're starting out on a stretch where we'll play ten games in 13 days. Before it's over, we'll have gone on the road and come home four different times. Chick Hearn says he can't remember a rougher piece of scheduling since the Lakers came to Los Angeles.

The regular season used to be 68 games long. Then it was increased to 72, then 80, and finally 82. Now, with exhibition games and with up to four rounds of playoffs, a championship

133

team could, theoretically at least, play 120 games before the season's over. Is it any wonder that when it finally ends, everybody just drops the ball and walks away? You're just burned out and need a rest.

But the funny thing is that even after a long regular season the quality of basketball in the playoffs is usually very good. It seems as if all the players shift gears so they'll be playing their best ball all the time. There's no more pacing yourself; you're playing for so much money that it becomes a tremendous incentive, and a lot of fun. No matter how tired you are, you want to keep playing because if the season ends early you haven't been successful. The season will last even longer this year because they've expanded the number of teams in the playoffs from eight to ten. The top two teams in each of the four divisions get in plus the best third-place team in each of the two conferences.

On the trip today I wore my usual traveling outfit: blue jeans, sports shirt, leather coat, tennis shoes. That's pretty close to what most of the others had on, except for Happy Hairston, who was wearing one of his tailor-made matching denim outfits, and the coaches, who had on sports coats. The Lakers don't make much of an issue of dress codes. As a matter of fact, there are fewer and fewer teams in the NBA with regulations about clothing. There seems to be a pattern to this. The clubs that have been strong for a number of years—the Lakers, the Knicks, the Bucks—are pretty much left alone. The expansion teams trying to build their organizations, though, do tend to require coats and ties. Steve Patterson, who plays for Cleveland, told me that since the Cavaliers didn't win many games they felt they couldn't afford to offend the public so they dressed conservatively.

When I was in Baltimore, the Bullets were somewhere in the middle. They were trying to win championships, trying to establish themselves as a class organization, so in the beginning they had a dress code requiring coats and ties. Then they got Mike Riordan from the Knicks, and he didn't even own a tie and refused to buy one. Well, the attitude of the team seemed to be, "Hell, he's from New York and they're a pretty good team so it must not be that important." One by one, the guys on the team started showing up without ties. There was supposed to be a $25 fine for that, but it got to be so ridiculous they let it slide. You got fined for not wearing a sports coat after that.

There is one big exception to this rule—the Boston Celtics, who have always had a rigid dress code. They all wear coats and ties, which can be a trip for a lot of the younger players. Many of them stopped wearing ties in college and a lot of times they travel in their suits with narrow lapels and their skinny high school ties. This isn't true for everybody, though. I have never seen Jo Jo White off the court when he hasn't been wearing a beautiful three-piece suit and a nice silk tie.

Curfews are another thing that have almost disappeared from professional basketball. The Bullets had a few, but I can't ever remember a bed check or anybody being fined for missing a curfew. The Lakers had one last year when we flew to Milwaukee for the start of the playoffs. And even then it was for midnight. It's not the same as football, where everybody is carefully bedded down for the night. I think this may be because there are fewer guys to control in basketball. And maybe football players by nature need somebody to watch out for them.

NOVEMBER 26

Now *that's* better. Better? Hell, it's great. Absolutely our best win of the year. We beat the Bucks 105–102 in Milwaukee despite a dynamite game by Kareem Abdul-Jabbar.

"I feel like we just won a world championship," Bill Sharman said afterward. That might be a little heavy, but we all felt pretty good about it. I had something to be happy about personally too. I finally got hot, and even though it only lasted for a quarter, at last I can say I made an offensive contribution. I had eight points, all in the first period, which helped us stay in a game that was close all the way. It really made me feel good when John Barnhill and Larry Creger told me I'd done well.

Which is not to say everything was perfect. In one play the Bucks worked a switch and I ended up guarding Abdul-Jabbar as he was driving. He just pushed me back and pushed me back and finally, when he had me off balance, shot over me and scored. There's no way you can stop that guy. I admit it. He's too good for me. And near the end of the game, when it was very close, I jumped up to get one of Kareem's shots that was rolling around the rim and about to come off. Just as I grabbed for it, the ball fell back through the hoop. Embarrassing.

Elmore Smith had an awful time with Abdul-Jabbar, who scored 36 points—25 in the first half and 16 in the first quarter when Elmore picked up three fouls trying to guard him. Zelmo Beaty came in early and did a little better against Kareem. He also scored well, getting 17 points, mostly on his little jumpers from eight or ten feet out. To tell you the truth, I think Elmore was just as happy to get out of there. Connie Hawkins did well coming off the bench, with 17 points, and Happy Hairston did a nice job on the boards with 17 rebounds. That's the way it is when a club plays a really good game. A lot of guys make contributions. It was nice to see us look like a team. One bad thing was that Gail Goodrich twisted an ankle in the third quarter when he stepped on Abdul-Jabbar's foot while driving and had to leave the game. We don't yet know how badly he is hurt.

The game was Kareem's first one at home since being out with his eye and hand injuries and he's wearing motorcycle-type goggles to protect his eyes. After the game he walked out of the arena wearing a leather helmet a fan had made for him. It had a strap under the chin and he looked like Snoopy going off to fight the Red Baron. It occurred to me that if he put his goggles on with the helmet he'd be ready to climb right into a Sopwith Camel. Nobody laughed at him, though. Hell, if you're Kareem Abdul-Jabbar, you could walk through the streets of Milwaukee naked and nobody with any sense would laugh.

NOVEMBER 27

This is one of those days I'd like to try all over again. From the top. As a matter of fact, I could have gotten along very nicely without it.

We flew to Kansas City early in the morning, and a few hours after we got here Kermit Washington laid the latest rumor on me. He said that Bill Sharman, John Barnhill, Larry Creger, and Chick Hearn had all gathered in a room and were calling around to find out if there was a forward available anywhere in the league.

Then, late in the afternoon, I had a talk with Connie Hawkins. He said that Bill had told him last night he'd be starting tonight against the Kings. "He came over to me after the game and said, 'What can we do to get you to play for us?'" the Hawk said. "I told him, 'Well, I can't come off the bench. I'm too old for that.' And he said, 'OK.'"

I felt rotten. A thousand things started going through my mind. I'd had three starts, and you really couldn't count one of those because of the foul situation. My defense, which was supposed to be the main thing I was to work on, had been all right, and yesterday I'd gotten going with shooting. And we'd *won* two of those games.

Then I thought, Yes, Connie *did* play well last night and

he *is* a streak player and he *should* be starting when he's going good. But why wouldn't Bill say something to me about it? Why let the Hawk tell me? Then it hit me. This is the way it was supposed to be all along. I'd never been anything more than bait for the Hawk. He was supposed to look at me starting, say to himself, "What's this shit?" and then really start putting out. It was the same thing as telling the other clubs during the exhibition season that Connie was available; the same thing as benching him and then playing him and then benching him again; the same thing as ripping him to the press. I was just something else they were trying to use to motivate him. I tried to put it all out of my mind. You can get paranoid if you dwell on this sort of thing. But what is it the man said? Even paranoids have enemies.

As it turned out, Bill never said a word to me about it. At the pregame meeting, when we discussed the Kings' players, he simply turned the floor over to Connie at one point and that's how everybody else found out. I could sense Elmore Smith and Kermit looking over at me, wondering what was going on. I was very grateful to the Hawk just then for having told me. I'd have hated to find out that way.

While we were in the locker room, the word spread around that Gail Goodrich hurt his ankle pretty badly last night. They've put it in a walking cast in Los Angeles and he'll be out for eight or nine games. It's a bad thing to happen to us right now, but surprisingly little was said about it. We're getting used to bad news, I guess.

Whatever might have been left of the euphoria over last night's win in Milwaukee disappeared in the second quarter against the Kings. They outscored us 33–15 and went on to beat us 107–89. None of us really played well in the first half, and the way things were going for the Kings was pretty much typified by a shot Nate Archibald made in the second period. He made a move slightly away from the basket to try to get off a turnaround jump shot, but Elmore was right behind him ready to crush the ball as soon as he let go of it. Now Nate is only 6-1; he gives away a whole foot to Elmore. But he was up in the air, had nobody to pass to, and would have been called

138

for traveling if he came down. So he just threw the ball up backward over his head in the general direction of the backboard. It went about 15 feet in the air and came straight down through the basket, touching nothing but net. Nobody could believe it, but as Nate started to run down to the other end of the floor, he just winked as if to say he knew what he was doing all the time.

At halftime I decided I just couldn't let what was happening go by without a comment. So I went up to Bill in the locker room and said I knew I hadn't done much coming off the bench in the first half, that I'd try harder the rest of the game, and that I felt we had a communication problem. He seemed freaked out that the game was going so badly after we'd played so well in Milwaukee and would only say that we'd talk about it later. That was no answer at all, of course, but I instantly felt a great deal better. Just to have brought it up, to have let him know it was weighing on me, made me feel less bugged about it.

I played better in the second half—though I only wound up with 20 minutes and eight points for the night—and so did the team as a whole. We were too far behind to catch up, but Bill mentioned after the game that we'd played better. One bright spot was Elmore, who had his best game so far: 19 points, 17 rebounds, four blocked shots. I think he was celebrating the fact that Abdul-Jabbar wasn't there tonight.

Our injury situation got even more ridiculous in the game. Lucius Allen banged up his leg and Kermit twisted his ankle when he stepped on somebody's foot. Poor Kermit. He's just getting over his back problems and starting to play a little and this has to happen.

We were back in the locker room after the game when the morning's rumor turned into the evening's reality. We were getting Corky Calhoun, a 6-7 forward from Phoenix, for two draft choices. His strong point is supposed to be defense. It isn't something that makes any of us feel secure. We can all count, and we know that if Cazzie Russell can come back this season we'll be one over the 12-man limit. And December 1, the deadline for cutting without having to pay somebody's full salary, is only four days away. There was very little said about getting Calhoun and none of the gallows humor among the forwards that might normally accompany it. Bill Bridges, who might have made some jokes about it, isn't even on the trip; he has bursitis in his right elbow. So we all just sat there for a while alone with our thoughts.

Kermit and I walked out to the bus and I looked over at him limping along. He gave a disgusted little smile and said, "I think I'm going to kill myself."

It was the only laugh I had all day.

NOVEMBER 29

Welcome to Medical Center. Pat Riley has an inflamed knee ligament. Lucius Allen has a bruised thigh. Happy Hairston has slivers of glass embedded in his foot. Kermit Washington has a twisted ankle. And those are some of the guys who *played* tonight.

On the bench before the game in street clothes were Gail Goodrich, Bill Bridges, and Cazzie Russell. We were lucky to win, even against New Orleans, which has won only two games all year. Pat scored 38 points—19 in the fourth quarter —bad knee and all. There's nothing like a game against Pete Maravich to help a guard's scoring average. At that, we only won by five points.

I hate to see guys play when they aren't up to it physically. And I see it a lot. I never liked it when Jerry West got shot up, and I don't like it when they do it to Elmore Smith. The shots deaden the pain, of course, but the reason the pain is there is that something is wrong. Deadening the pain and continuing to play is only going to make it worse.

I am convinced, for instance, that Willis Reed would still

be around if he hadn't played against the Lakers in the final round of the playoffs of the 1969–1970 season after injuring his knee. The legend, of course, is that Reed's presence in the lineup gave the Knicks such an emotional lift that they won the championship. That may be true. But it is also true that he never played a full season again, and after several knee operations he had to retire this year at the age of 32.

Wes Unseld was another one who played injured all the time. When I was with the Bullets, his knees were in terrible shape—tendinitis, pulled ligaments, the whole show—but they would shoot his knees up with cortisone, wrap a mile of tape around them, and send him out there hardly able to move. There was a lot of pressure from management because they needed him. He was young and strong and effective even when he was playing hurt. But doing it might have shortened his career. Once, when they were taping him up before a game, I said, "Wesley, you are going to kill yourself. You are going to wreck your knees."

"I've got to do it," was all he said. I got the impression he knew he was making a mistake but felt it was his job to do what he was told. The strange thing was there were guys on the team who thought he was kissing up to management by playing when he was hurt.

Gus Johnson's situation on the Bullets was different. Gus could jump out of the gym when he was healthy, but his knees had been operated on several times and he really wasn't very effective any more. Gus would be pretty banged up when the regular season was over. So he'd tell Gene Shue he couldn't play in the playoffs. Shue would tell Abe Pollin, the Bullets' owner, who would go to Gus and say, here's a few bucks. Go play tonight as a favor. And he'd give him a couple of thousand dollars. This happened twice that I know of—once the year I was drafted by the Bullets and once my first year with them. At the time, I thought it was a pretty good move on Pollin's part, that maybe some extra motivation was what Gus needed. But it turned out that Gus would play a game—and not very well; you could tell he was hurting—and then miss the next two because his knees would be killing him.

One funny thing happened tonight: The University of Southern California opened its basketball season, and its games are broadcast on the same radio station ours are on. So they recorded our game and played it when the Trojan game was over, which means we didn't come on until almost 10:30 P.M. USC gets preferred treatment because it signed its contract with the radio station first—the Lakers were on a different station last year—but it almost seems like a comment on the way we're playing.

I suppose our fans must hate it, but I kind of enjoyed going home to listen to Chick Hearn call the game. Tonight is the first time I've ever really heard him. He really is a brilliant play-by-play announcer. Chick talks so fast he can literally follow the ball around the court, keeping up with everybody who gets a hand on it. But when he starts commenting on the game and analyzing it, he's still talking fast, and it's as if he doesn't have time to think about what he's saying. So he really exaggerates and builds things up. Everything is either the greatest play he ever saw or the worst.

At one point in the game the referee called a technical foul on me and I got mad at myself and said, "God damn it!", bawling myself out. But the ref was walking right by me as I said it and he thought I was swearing at him so he called the technical.

It really bugged me to get a T for such a common curse that had been meant for myself and I told the ref, "At least let me get a few good words in on you."

DECEMBER 1

We beat Phoenix tonight 111–105 in our first overtime game of the season. It was an important win because we lost to the Warriors in Oakland last night and fell six games behind them. The schedule is beginning to catch up with us; second place and a playoff spot may be the most we can hope for unless there's a drastic improvement.

Tonight's game was the best example yet of why the Lakers keep bugging Elmore Smith and trying to figure out how to get him to produce. Elmore was incredible. He played 50 of the 53 minutes, scored 29 points, had 20 rebounds, and blocked nine shots. And he was playing against Dennis Awtrey, who's a good, physical center. Elmore's potential is just so awesome he could turn us around all by himself if he could just play this way consistently.

The Hawk really flew tonight too. Connie started but couldn't get going at all in the first half, so Bill Sharman took him out. In the fourth quarter he went back in, without having scored a single point, and went berserk. He scored 16 points in the quarter and the overtime period. It was vintage Connie Hawkins, the way he must have looked on the playgrounds. He took every kind of shot imaginable, with guys hanging all over him, and he just couldn't miss.

Corky Calhoun played his first game as a Laker, substituting for Connie and Happy Hairston, and he ended up with 43 minutes, more than anybody on the team except Elmore. He scored ten points and had five rebounds. Bill praised his defense after the game. I played 12 minutes, scored nine points, and had seven rebounds.

More trouble for Pat Riley. His thumb popped out of joint and just flopped around on his hand. It's one of those freak injuries that can keep you out for a week or correct itself in a minute. Luckily, Pat's thumb popped back into place right away. If we lose him, we may be hard pressed to muster a quorum pretty soon.

DECEMBER 2

This is *not* the way to begin a trip to the East. If I believed in omens, I would say we were going to have trouble. First, neither Bill Bridges nor Happy Hairston made the trip. Bill's bursitis is still bothering him, and Happy has come down with tendinitis in his knee. It's interesting to observe Happy in this kind of situation. To me, it seems that a lot of it is psychological, almost a bid for attention. When everything is going well, he has no sign of any knee trouble or foot trouble. It's only when things are not going right that his injuries become prominent. That's when he'll start grabbing his knee and wincing in pain. Most of the players on the team hate seeing him go through this; it brings us down just when we're trying our hardest to get things together. But Happy is such a key element of the team that you have to put up with it.

Another thing is that Connie Hawkins missed the plane from Los Angeles to New York. That makes him 0 for 2. He also missed the plane to Oakland two days ago. I don't think Bill Sharman is very happy about it.

Then, when we got to New York, there was a screwup in our bags. It took an hour to get them off the plane, and Elmore Smith had checked his through on the wrong airline. We were all pretty pissed by the time we got on the bus to the hotel.

And the hotel! I've had small rooms before, especially in New York, but this is unbelievable. The bed takes up half the space, and when I open up the suitcase it's impossible to walk around the room. I started to laugh when I thought about all these huge basketball players crammed into tiny hotel rooms like Fred Allen's hunchbacked mice.

I decided to order some room service. A sandwich, a malt, and a piece of cantaloupe cost $12 and the guy looked at me funny when I only tipped him a buck. Elmore told me he had a $22 room service bill just for himself and when he gave the bellman a couple of dollars, the guy said, "Hell, that isn't even 10 percent."

"Well, kiss my ass," Elmore told him. "You better get out of here. I spend $22 and you want me to give you . . ." The guy took off pretty fast.

How can anybody live in this city?

DECEMBER 3

Playing in Madison Square Garden is a trip. I think it's the most tremendous feeling in basketball. There are always 19,000 people there, and they're so much into the game that the atmosphere seems to be more highly charged than most places. The fans are completely for the Knicks, of course, but even the visiting teams seem to get a boost from them and play their best, most competitive basketball.

Lucius Allen, with 33 points, and Pat Riley, with 20, did more than half of our scoring; we shot only 42 percent from the floor, but the amazing thing is we were in the game right to the end. We lost 100–95, and the Knicks pulled it out only because Phil Jackson hit his last ten shots and had 22 points, his season high. I played for 26 minutes, had 11 points, and thought I did all right on defense against Harthorne Wingo. He had eight points and I don't think he had more than one basket in the fourth quarter.

All in all, it was a pretty good team performance considering we are without our top scorer and our top rebounder and are still getting used to the moves of two new players. Once we get Gail Goodrich and Happy Hairston back, we could be all right. Bill Sharman was mad as hell, though. He kept the locker room closed for 20 minutes and told us we weren't prepared and we weren't thinking about basketball. Then he looked over at Connie Hawkins and said very loudly, "By the way, if you miss another plane, it's going to cost you $1,000."

It was the first time I've ever heard Bill chew a guy out in front of the whole team. I think the pressure of all the losses is starting to build on him. He's beginning to realize we may not get in the playoffs—or even make a good run at them— if we lose too many more. But taking it out on Connie for missing a plane seems pointless. I think Bill may have been more upset over the Hawk's scoring only four points tonight.

In the Knicks' dressing room Walt Frazier told Rich Levin, "They're not the same Lakers any more. I sleep much better the night before we play them knowing I don't have to guard Jerry West. I sort of miss playing them without West and Wilt Chamberlain. We had a good rivalry going. They have no punch and the offense is just set up for the guards."

That's Walt Frazier talking, gang. I think he summed it up pretty well. The day hasn't been a total loss, though. At least we're getting out of New York.

DECEMBER 4

We got into Boston about two this morning and Lucius Allen, Connie Hawkins, and I decided to walk over to a coffee shop near the hotel to get something to eat. Instead of being empty, the way you would expect at that time of night, the place was really jumping. It looked as if every hooker and pimp in town was there, getting in out of the cold.

"Oh, yeah," the Hawk kidded when he saw what was going on. "I am eating *here*. Hey, will somebody loan me some money?" A few of the guys in the coffee shop recognized the Hawk and gave him a "What's happening, man?" So we sat around eating sandwiches and talking to what seemed like the whole cast of *Super Fly*. Life is never dull when you're with the Hawk.

Looking around at all those women was pretty interesting. Professional athletes are great women chasers—and women catchers—but it's not always that easy to score. Sure, there are players who have girls waiting for them in a lot of cities, but when you're only in town from 24 to 36 hours, a girl really has to be dedicated. You can always import one, of course, have her travel to the city you're playing in, but that can get to be expensive.

In some ways, I think, athletes in other sports have it a little easier. Baseball players get to a town and stay there for three or four days. And when a football player has a Sunday game on the road, he usually leaves for it on Thursday or Friday. He has some time on his hands, whereas a basketball player is usually in town for only one day, and half the time he's either playing or practicing. So if a baseball or football player meets a girl, he can say, "Let's go have dinner. Let's go have lunch. Let's go to a show." About all a basketball player can say is, "Let's go to my room."

This can make it kind of hard to impress a good-looking girl. And that part of it is very important. So much of women chasing is status. Most guys would rather stay in their room than be seen with a pig. And as for the girls who run after ballplayers, well, even if they're attractive a lot of them are pretty weird. They're almost like scalp hunters, in a way. Once last year Cheryl was waiting for me at the Forum after a game and somebody introduced her to a girl who was hanging around. "Oh, you're Stan Love's girlfriend," she said. "I have a friend who fucked————," and she named one of the Laker players. Isn't that charming?

What it boils down to is this: if a basketball player is looking for women he generally has to *look*. In Baltimore we once made up a mythical All-Lobby team, consisting of guys who spent every available hour sitting in hotel lobbies talking to the women who came by, trying to get something going. There are generally two or three guys on each team like this. On the Lakers, however, there are no contenders for All-Lobby status. Very seldom do you actually *see* anybody with a strange woman. Whatever happens takes place either in the player's room or away from the hotel. I think it may all be another part of the Laker image: you just don't want to put yourself in the position of being seen doing something you could be criticized for.

Anyway, no matter how well athletes do, I'll always believe that rock musicians get more ladies. The girls who go to rock concerts are much more liberal; they're all in one room, and 90 percent of them are turned on to begin with.

More of the same tonight. Damn, but it's frustrating. Here we are a crippled team, in the middle of a brutal stretch of the schedule, playing good clubs on the road . . . and almost winning. Almost.

We were really excited at the prospect of beating Boston in its own arena underneath all those world championship banners that make visiting teams cringe. It's the same feeling I had at Oregon when the team came in to play UCLA and got a look at all the NCAA championship flags hanging from the rafters. We actually led the Celtics going into the fourth quarter and stayed right with them until the end, when they scored 13 of the last 15 points in the game to beat us by 11. They just got us thinking, Hey, we can get these guys. Then it's as if they said, "OK, time to go to work," and they went out and crushed us. I've seen that kind of mentality at work before. It's what the Lakers used to do several years ago.

Poor Elmore Smith. Dave Cowens ate him up alive. He scored 32 points, had 15 rebounds, and just pushed Elmore around wherever he wanted him to go. Whenever Elmore tried to occupy a position, Cowens was already there. Elmore finished with only six points and really felt bad.

Considering his size (6-9), I think Cowens may be the best center in basketball. He can get the same 30 points and 20 rebounds that Kareem Abdul-Jabbar can, but he'll also run with you more and move the ball around. For sure, a guy like Cowens makes for a more interesting type of game. At least a lot of the players I've talked to think so. He doesn't just hang around under the basket. When you're guarding Abdul-Jabbar, you run from one end of the court to the other and then try to guard him at that one position he wants, which is on the left side down low, for his sky hook. But with Cowens you've got to watch yourself because one minute he might be over in the corner shooting a 20-footer on you and the next minute he might be right underneath the basket. The same is true with Bob McAdoo. He can pop up anywhere on the court. You're also more involved in the game when you're playing opposite a guy like that. At least you *feel* you can be a factor in the game against Cowens. I just can't describe the difference between guarding a guy who's 6-9 and one who's 7-4. Kareem makes you feel so inadequate that it seems as if you're not playing the same game he is.

Near the end of the game Cowens and Kermit Washington traded a few punches under the backboard. It could have been a hell of a fight because Kermit is almost as tall as Cowens and they both weigh 230. But they were separated and thrown out of the game before anybody could do any real damage.

It's unusual to see real brawls in basketball, which is probably just as well because somebody could really get hurt. It isn't like football or hockey, where everybody's wearing pads, and there are some big strong guys in this game. That may be the reason most fights don't get very far, in fact. In Baltimore we had a couple of policemen. Gus Johnson could even up sides in a hurry if one of the Bullets was getting pounded on, so just his presence tended to keep things cool.

Wes Unseld had the same effect. Once, when I was with the Bullets, Mel Counts, who played for Phoenix at the time, wanted to fight me. Mel is one of the nicest people I've ever met, by the way, but he is also 7-0 and weighs 235, so I wasn't especially eager to get into anything with him. Luckily, Wes stepped in between us and said, "If you try to get him, I'm going to get you and a few others." Mel walked away and I said, "Thank you, Wesley. That was very nice of you."

Sometimes fights break out because one guy is hot and the player guarding him is frustrated. One night the Bullets were playing the Knicks in Baltimore and Jack Marin was having a great game, really giving Phil Jackson a hard time. As we were coming down the court at one point, Phil changed directions suddenly and waited for Jack near the side of the court. Then he just belted him and knocked him over the press table into an aisle on the other side. Jack jumped right back over the table and started swinging. They got into a pretty good fight before it was finally broken up.

But the worst fight I have ever seen in basketball happened when the Lakers were in Seattle last season. It started between Bill Bridges, 6-6, 235, and Spencer Haywood, 6-8, 230. Bill was guarding Haywood and had his hands on him a lot, which really bugged him. Haywood kept pushing Bill's hands down and once he did it pretty hard when they were in front of the Seattle bench. They squared off and Haywood knocked Bill down with a punch. The whole Seattle bench just jumped on Bill and started clobbering him until the refs pulled them off.

When Bill started walking away, Haywood suddenly came after him again and they started fighting at midcourt. Mahdi Abdul-Rahman (he changed his name from Walt Hazzard) jumped on Bill from behind and started to choke him. Bill just flipped him over his back, slammed him on the floor, and fell on top of him. John Brisker came over and started kicking Bill in the head. Finally, the refs got everybody separated for good and kicked Bill and Haywood out of the game.

The amazing thing about the fight is that Bill was the only Laker in it. It started down at the other end of the court, about 90 feet away from our bench, but even the guys out on the floor who were only a few feet away when the Seattle players began coming at Bill didn't make any move to restrain them. In the locker room after the game Bill was crying and yelling, "How come none of you sons of bitches helped me out?! Why did you let me get my head kicked in?!"

It made me feel terrible and I tried to say something about being so far away and how it had all happened so fast. But I wondered too why the guys in the game didn't try to help. You don't expect your prize guards, the little guys, to get into something like that, but maybe your big, strong rebounding forward and your center could have pushed people away. The more I thought about it, the more I began to think that it was really typical of the Lakers. Everybody is into his own thing so much, trying to develop his own LA image to the exclusion of the other players, that nobody has any time or any thoughts for anybody else. In the end, we all get selfish. Selfish when a guy gets in trouble and selfish when we play the game. I'm starting to see it in myself too. And I don't like it.

DECEMBER 5

I was sitting with Rich Levin during the plane ride home this morning and I handed him one of the Boston papers. A guy covering last night's game had written that we weren't the real Lakers but imposters in Los Angeles uniforms.

"Hand it up to Chick," I said as Rich finished reading it. He passed it to Chick Hearn, who was sitting in front of us with Larry Creger.

"Hey, Chick, read this," Rich said, and we settled back to wait for the explosion.

"This guy went a little too far," Chick said and he ripped the article out of the paper. "I'm going to show this to Jack Kent Cooke."

Another story in the paper said Bill Walton was considering quitting basketball. He's been out of the Portland lineup with a foot injury and I guess it really bothers him. Also, the article speculated that he hates the travel and all the press conferences his first time around the league. Just about everybody on the team had an opinion about it and the comments were surprisingly mixed. You heard everything from "More power to him" to "The guy's an idiot."

Both Elmore Smith and Brian Winters were quite sympathetic to Walton's doubts about what he'd gotten himself into. "The guy should be able to do what he wants to do," Elmore said. "If he doesn't love basketball, why should he play?" I think he might have been talking about himself as much as about Bill Walton.

"Maybe he just doesn't want to play basketball," Brian said.

"Well, what else can he do?" I said. "I don't care what kind of principles or values you have. You can't exist today without a few bucks. Idealistically, it may be great to throw it all away and go live in the hills somewhere, but it's not very relevant to what's happening. The guy could play for three years and have enough to live the rest of his life doing whatever he wants. We all have to work a little bit, produce something." My God, I thought, I'm turning Establishment in my old age.

It went on for quite a while, and even though I doubt any of us really thought Walton would walk out on a $3 million contract, nobody could blame him for thinking about it. There are times when all of us feel we'd love never to see another basketball again.

DECEMBER 6

I knew something was wrong the minute I walked into the locker room for the shootaround this morning. Nobody had to say anything; I could feel it in the atmosphere of the room. It seemed to be bouncing off the walls. I waited a second and looked around, trying to figure out what it was. Then Connie Hawkins told me. The Lakers had cut Bill Bridges.

I got a little light-headed for a minute and went over to my locker so I could sit on my stool and try to make some sense out of it. I looked over at Bill's locker and saw that it was not only empty but clean. Somebody must have dusted it. The plastic name tag had been removed. There was nothing to indicate that anybody had ever used it, not the slightest hint that articles had once been stored there belonging to a human being.

153

Somebody told me we had acquired Stu Lantz from New Orleans for some unannounced future draft pick. He was flying in from Seattle today and would be in uniform tonight. My mind was racing, trying to figure out (1) the rationale for the deal, (2) what would happen to Bill, and (3) what it meant to the rest of us. From the few conversations I had, it appeared that nobody was doing much better at figuring it out than I was.

Lantz is a guard, an experienced veteran, but a guard. They are cutting a forward, a position where we are having trouble, and adding a guard, where we're overloaded. Why? As for Bill, well, he's been hurt, he's 35, and he's slowed down a little, but he's still a good man to have around, especially in certain defensive situations. He's one of only ten players in NBA history with 10,000 points and 10,000 rebounds. He's also a good man who keeps everybody loose and who is everybody's friend. It's hard to think he won't be around any more.

And the rest of us? Bill's being cut makes us have to think about the unthinkable again. The roster is full. The cast is off Cazzie Russell's leg. He's talking about being able to play again by the middle of January. Something is going to have to give. Or rather, somebody.

Then it hit me. What day is this? The sixth? I smiled to myself. Bill had beaten the cut deadline by less than a week. They have to pay him for the whole season.

Pete Newell must be a genius. For one night at least. Stu Lantz caught a 7:00 A.M. plane from Seattle, where New Orleans had last played, arrived late for the shootaround, practiced with us a little, went out and found a place to stay, and came back to the Forum tonight and scored 26 points. He was 11 for 13 from the floor, and we crushed Atlanta 108–84. How does that theory about getting used to the guys you're playing with go again?

Should I add that I didn't play tonight? Why bother?

DECEMBER 7

Stu Lantz returned to earth tonight in Phoenix (5 for 11 from the floor for ten points) and so did we. The Suns beat us 92–88 and moved ahead of us into fourth place. We're back in the cellar. It was an all-time weird game. We did not score a basket for four minutes in the second period and then again for eight minutes in the third, and we *still* only lost by four. Which shows how Phoenix played, I guess. The game was incredibly sloppy on both sides.

The most interesting thing was what went on between Happy Hairston and Richie Powers in the third quarter. Happy thought he was fouled underneath and yelled at Powers for not calling it. So Richie, who is a good official but sort of a little peacock, strutting around on the court, called a technical foul on Happy, who just went berserk. He ran up to Richie, put his face right up (or I should say down) at his, and yelled as loud as he could. Richie stood there and even leaned forward a little bit to challenge Happy, to see what he would do. Happy leaned forward too and they wound up bumping into each other a couple of times. I don't think I've ever seen a player and a referee going at it that hard. Finally, Richie threw Happy out of the game, which might have been just as well. It may be about as angry as I've ever seen Happy. Or anybody else.

The pressure can get to you in so many ways.

DECEMBER 8

Before the game tonight—another one with the Suns, this time in the Forum—Keith Erickson, a Phoenix forward, came up to me and said, "What's happening to you, Love? Are they hiding you?" We laughed, but I didn't have an answer. We beat Phoenix this time 107–102, and though Bill Sharman used a lot of strange lineups, none of them included me. That's three straight games I haven't been in. No sign of that discussion Bill promised me in Kansas City ten days or so ago either. I think it's up to him this time. I don't know what more I can do or say.

Stu Lantz played at forward tonight along with Happy Hairston, and Kermit Washington played center. It made sense, in a way: two good rebounders and a third guard in the lineup. It's what Gene Shue liked to do to get the running game going. The only problem is it didn't work. We were up by ten points before the half, and by the end of the third quarter Phoenix was ahead. It wasn't until Elmore Smith and two legitimate forwards went back in that we took the lead to stay.

Bill has pretty much junked his normal pattern of rotating three forwards, three guards, and two centers and is just juggling the lineup around every which way. With Gail Goodrich still out with his ankle injury—he may be back for our next game, in five days—we've really been lacking stability. Fortunately, Lucius Allen has been coming on strong. He's getting a lot of points and doing a fine job quarterbacking the team. I think it's turned into a very good trade for us.

Lucius came over to the house for lunch the other day,

and it made me feel good just to listen to him talk about how happy he is. In Milwaukee all they wanted him to do was set up Kareem Abdul-Jabbar. Nobody can know, he said, how great it is not to hear Larry Costello yelling at him all the time to get it in to the big guy.

It's awfully nice watching Lucius play. He really penetrates, bursting up the middle to draw the defense toward him the way Jerry West did. He creates shots for himself and everybody else and that's what we need from him. His game is unselfish. He's so quick he can beat defenders to wherever he wants to go. He's so controlled, yet so fast. His attitude toward the player guarding him seems to be, "Come and get me if you can," and if the guy isn't quick about it, Lucius will have the ball in the basket. But when his man stays with him, he gets rid of the ball, finds the open man.

"It's just so nice to be able to do what I want, to be able to play my game," he said. "It's really good for my career to be here. But sometimes I think it might be bad playing in LA."

"What do you mean?" I asked him.

"It's just such a nice city," he said, "that it takes a lot of work to stay sharp and keep your mind on basketball."

What a nice problem to have, I thought.

DECEMBER 10

Bill Bridges called today. It was the first time we've had a chance to talk since he was cut and it was good just to be able to kid around with him. Things have really changed on the Lakers since he left. Nobody seems to be having fun any more. And there aren't any more jokes about getting traded or cut. It was Bill who made that kind of joke and the fact that he got cut himself brought it home to everybody.

The team seems very impersonal now. The closeness we had last year and at the beginning of this season just isn't there. There are a lot of new guys now and, well, I'm just not as close to Corky Calhoun as I was to Bill. Hell, I barely even *know* Corky Calhoun. Also, we're being pushed apart by all the turmoil, the comings and goings. There's just so much insecurity. Connie Hawkins really acts bugged, for instance. And when good-natured guys like the Hawk get bugged, you can imagine what it's like with people who aren't all that friendly to begin with. Elmore Smith and I are becoming distant too. He's unhappy and moody. He plays tremendous basketball for three or four games and then he doesn't. I don't know what it is, but I can tell he's bothered by something.

Then, of course, there's the fact that we're losing. I'm sure that has a lot to do with it. Everybody's very quiet, working very hard, not saying anything, not laughing about anything. The pressure's on and we've got to win. That's the atmosphere now and we all feel it.

Anyway, Bill told me to just stay loose, that eventually I'd get in there.

"What are you going to do?" I asked him.

"Well, Seattle said they're interested and I've talked to Phoenix, but I think I'm going to forget it. I'm kind of tired. I think I'm ready to retire."

It's not so bad, I thought later. Bill doesn't need the money, I'm sure, and he's never lived very flamboyantly to begin with, not like some of the guys in the game. Like Wilt Chamberlain and the house he had built for himself with everything designed to fit a seven-footer. Or Walt Frazier and his incredible wardrobe. Or Nate Thurmond and his fleet of expensive cars. When Gus Johnson was with the Bullets, he had 300 pairs of shoes, including some $200 alligators. Every time we went to New York, he would carry so much cash that he couldn't fold it and put it in his pocket. He had to carry it flat and keep it all together with a rubber band. It must have been at least a couple of thousand dollars. There certainly are some classic characters in this game.

The Knicks won their sixth straight game today. It's really a tribute to those guys to be able to lose a Reed, a DeBusschere, and a Lucas in one year and still be right in it with teams like Buffalo and Boston in their division. It's a tremendous accomplishment, I think. One thing I'm really happy to see is the way Phil Jackson has come on. He's been there seven years now, and for a while he didn't play much. They said he was awkward and clumsy and played bad defense, but he's hung around long enough to work himself into a reasonable role on the team and to contribute. It gives me hope.

DECEMBER 13

Elmore Smith said something very interesting after the game tonight. We beat Seattle 109–93, and Elmore had another one of those excellent games he's capable of: 19 points, 23 rebounds, 8 for 12 from the floor, several blocked shots. Rich Levin asked him about it and Elmore said, "It's a funny thing. You feel like you are playing hard all the time, but then you realize nothing is getting done so you've got to find out what you are doing wrong." That is the most introspective thing about basketball I've ever heard Elmore say. It may be that he's starting to realize how his personal life affects his playing and is determined to do something about it.

Gail Goodrich returned to the lineup tonight after missing eight games with his ankle injury. It took him about two seconds to find the range. He scored 26 points, hit 50 percent from the floor, and teamed up with Lucius Allen as if they'd been playing together all their lives. Lucius scored 30 points and he and Gail had 19 assists between them. Bill Sharman told the press that they complement each other the way Gail and Jerry West did. It's conceivable that if Gail stays healthy and Cazzie Russell comes back strong, we'll still have a shot at the playoffs. For all our troubles, we're only two and a half games out of second place now.

Happy Hairston missed the game because of his injured knee. One other forward didn't play either. That's four straight games on the bench.

DECEMBER 15

Remember that unbelievable game against Chicago last month where we scored only 76 points? Well, forget it. Today's game was worse. We played in Portland, the nationally televised Sunday afternoon game, and in the first half we killed the Trail Blazers. Just blew them out. No contest. Elmore Smith was fantastic, gobbling up every rebound in sight; and at halftime we led 64–38. At one point early in the second half we were ahead by 27 points. And then we lost. It was absolutely shocking. I've never seen anything like it.

Guys like Geoff Petrie and Barry Clemens and Lloyd Neal just started chipping away at us and we couldn't stop them. The strange thing was that we couldn't even see it coming until it was too late. We were still ahead by 18 at the beginning of the fourth quarter and we weren't really worried. But they kept hitting and we kept missing and the crowd kept hollering like crazy. With five minutes to go Portland was within five points and finally caught us and won by three.

How can a team score 36 points in the second quarter and 33 in the second *half?* I wish I knew. The 24-second clock is part of it, of course. You can't just sit on a lead; you have to keep shooting. And when you're not scoring and the other team is, things can turn around in a hurry. It becomes psychological after a while too. You just get the *feeling* that you're not going to score and that you can't stop the other team's momentum. You *know* they're going to hit and you're not. So you start to press, to force shots, and the ball feels like iron in your hand. It happens in a lot of NBA games; that's why so many of them go right down to the end. But it usually doesn't last for an entire half. Eventually, the other team has to stop making every shot and you have to start hitting some of yours. But not today. It was just incredible.

My magic number is now five. I'm not sure, but that may be as long as I've ever gone without playing.

DECEMBER 17

I'm not sure I know the best way to describe what happened tonight. Maybe if I just start at the beginning . . .

We lost to Cleveland by 13 points at the Forum; we were ahead until the fourth quarter, when the Cavaliers outscored us by 14 points. I didn't play for the sixth straight time. I was walking out of the tunnel after the game and had stopped to sign an autograph when I saw my brother Steve.

"Again, huh?" he said. "You want me to talk to him?"

"Yeah, go ahead," I said, and I pointed behind me. "He's back there."

"No, he's not. He just walked by." Steve started walking after Bill Sharman.

I went home, where Cheryl was making dinner for Steve Patterson of the Cavaliers, his wife, Marilyn, and me. We were sitting around chatting when my brother Steve came over. He said he had caught up with Bill in the parking lot and had walked with him all the way over to the Hyatt House on the other side of the street, about three-quarters of a mile away. All the while they were walking, Steve said, he tried to talk to Bill, but without much success. Finally, on the sidewalk outside the hotel, Steve got Bill to stop for 10 or 15 minutes. He told him we were both disappointed that I wasn't being given a chance to play, reminded him that my statistics had been good, and repeated some of the things we'd said earlier in the season about how hard I was trying to work, how much I wanted to help the team.

It was probably a bad time for this. We had just lost a tough game, were back in last place in the division, and Bill was clearly bugged by the way things were going. But the situation has stayed the same for so long now that Steve thought he should try to start some kind of communication. It was some kind, all right. Bill told Steve I didn't have "a feel for the game." Whatever that means. Steve pressed the point, asking him what he meant, and Bill said some more things. They all added up to this: I don't know how to play basketball. It is, I suppose, the worst thing a coach can say about a player.

Steve really got mad and said, "I can understand your using Stan to motivate Connie Hawkins. But don't give me that bullshit that Stan can't play the game." Bill just freaked out over that, of course. The conversation grew pretty heated. Bill eventually got very quiet and said, "Tell Stan to come in before practice tomorrow and we will go over everything again."

I've got to get out of here. I know that now. I've got to go someplace where I can play offensive basketball, someplace where they're not talking about defense all the time, someplace where the guards aren't the only ones who are supposed to shoot.

But first I'm going to do what Bill told Steve I should do. I'm going to see him in the morning and try to have this out.

DECEMBER 18

Practice was scheduled for 11:00 A.M. today and I went in half an hour early. Bill Sharman wasn't there, though, so I caught him afterward.

"What's wrong?" I said. "What has happened?"

"Be patient," Bill said. "I'm trying to play different combinations. I've got 11 other guys bugging me to play too."

How strange, I thought. He tells Steve I can't play. He tells me to be patient. Doesn't he think we talk to each other?

"If we keep losing," Bill said, "it's going to reach a point this season where I'm going to have to bench the older guys and start going with the younger ones."

Is *that* it? I thought. Am I supposed to hope we keep *losing* so I'll get some playing time? This is too much.

"Bill," I said, "is it in your mind that I can't play for you?"

"Practice harder," he said, "show me that you can outhustle these guys."

It was hard for me to keep from groaning. Almost half a season has gone by and he's still looking at who runs up and down the court the fastest in practice. At this point everybody is taking it a little easier, saving it for the games. If you go all out every time you step on the floor, whether for a practice or for a game, you'll be four feet tall at the end of the season. And the reserves can't practice like maniacs when the starters, the players they're guarding, are only going through the motions.

"OK," I said. "I will." And I walked away.

What a shambles this season has become. What a shame.

DECEMBER 20

We led Detroit by nine points with eight minutes to go tonight but lost by a point. The paid attendance at the Forum was 9,667, the lowest of the season. I sat out my seventh straight game. Pat Riley didn't play either, and he's been so effective at times coming off the bench and scoring. I don't understand it. But I repeat myself.

I found myself thinking tonight about the difference between sitting on the bench for a team that is winning and for one that is losing. There's just such a different atmosphere. When you're winning, everybody's happy: the front office, the coaches, the players. Everybody feels like part of things. And when you're winning all the time, you're usually blowing teams out so everybody gets a chance to play, to stay sharp, to keep his head together.

Some of the guys who were around three years ago, during the Lakers' 33-game winning streak, said there wasn't a guy on the team who didn't make an important contribution at one time or another. It wasn't just seven or eight guys. Flynn Robinson came off the bench a couple of times and scored some key points, and John Q. Trapp was a big factor in reserve. In fact, when you looked back on the win streak, there wasn't a single guy on the team you couldn't point to and say, "Without him, the streak would have ended earlier."

Jim Cleamons, the Lakers' number-one draft choice that season, got in just 38 games and averaged about five minutes of playing time and 2.6 points a game. Los Angeles traded him to Cleveland for a draft choice at the end of the year. And when the Cavaliers beat us three nights ago, guess who their leading scorer was? Jim stepped right in for Austin Carr, who's been hurt, and got his career high, 29 points. How sweet it must have been for him.

DECEMBER 21

When the streak ended tonight, when I finally got into a game, I felt no emotion. None.

There were three minutes left to play in Phoenix and the game was lost when Bill Sharman called my name. So I went in and tried to shake the rust off my bones. I had no idea I would be called on and found it hard to relate what I was doing to any kind of basketball. It wasn't even practice, really. You wouldn't run out and jump right into a practice without thinking about what you were going to do or warming up for a minute. It was very clear they expected nothing from me and that's about what they got.

The Suns beat us by ten points; it was our fourth straight loss. In those four games we have been outscored by an average of 18 points in the second half. In fact, lately we have led most of our games at halftime and have lost anyhow. Which means we are letting down, not fighting. I don't think we have ever missed Jerry West more. He was the greatest I've ever seen at playing tough when the pressure was on.

Pat Riley played for a few minutes too, after missing the last two games. I was sitting next to him in the locker room before the game when Bill came over to him and said he wanted to talk to him. They must have spoken for 20 minutes before Pat came out on the floor.

When I asked Pat what it was, he looked at me funny and said, "Shit, someday I'll tell you."

I don't think I want to hear it, to tell you the truth.

DECEMBER 23

We were down by five points at halftime against Portland last night and a few guys joked kind of quietly that maybe it was a good sign after losing all those games we'd been leading at the half. And I'll be damned if it wasn't. We ripped the Trail Blazers in the second half and won 115–102. Gail Goodrich went wild with 44 points, his highest total of the season. It felt good to be off the skids. I played three minutes again.

There was a surprise among all the Christmas cards in the mail today: a letter from my mother. My folks only live about half an hour down the freeway from here, in Cypress, but she said she wanted to write something down.

Steve and Mike and I told them on Thanksgiving that we were picking up the payments on their house, and Mom wrote that she had already noticed the difference in Dad. He has worked hard for so many years. Now he won't have to worry about the day-to-day grind so much. He can use his money to go to Europe and buy other things he wants. Laker tickets, maybe.

DECEMBER 25

Ah, to be in Cleveland now that Christmas is here.

We flew in today and went straight to the arena to practice. Then I dashed over to Steve Patterson's house for a late dinner. It's really nice to have friends on other teams if only because it keeps you from being lonelier on the road than you might otherwise be. You play, you eat, you sleep, you wake up, you drive to the airport, you catch a plane, you fly to the next city, you go to the hotel, you change clothes, you go to the arena, you shoot around, you go back to the hotel, you take a nap, you wake up at five, you go to the arena, you play the next game, and on and on. A lot of times you wake up on the road and think, Where the hell am I? It takes a while before you remember what city you're in. It can be so nice just to spend a few hours with a friend.

Steve and I have known each other since high school, when we played in tournaments together. I like to tease him that he is the answer to the sports trivia question: "Who played center on the two NCAA championship teams UCLA had after Lew Alcindor but before Bill Walton?" Having dinner with Steve and Marilyn sure beat hotel turkey.

DECEMBER 27

What a funny game this is. Just when things are at their worst and you think the season is lost, you score two good wins over tough teams on the road. We beat Cleveland 99–89 last night (Kermit Washington had his best game of the season: 11 points, nine rebounds) and then ripped Chicago tonight 105–93 (Lucius Allen scored 37 points, two short of his NBA high). Tonight, for the first time in a long while, I felt like part of the team.

We were ahead of the Bulls by 15 points at halftime, but they cut it down to just two with eight minutes left. The big crowd was hollering and things looked pretty bad. Then I heard Bill Sharman call my name. I was surprised because I didn't play last night and haven't been in a game in a key situation in an awfully long time. The first time I got my hands on the ball I hit a jump shot, and a few moments later I went up for another one and was fouled. I missed one of the free throws, but those three points gave us some breathing room and got us started again.

An amazing statistic. This is the first time this season we've won three games in a row. Everybody felt great. "I think we are getting used to one another," Happy Hairston told Rich Levin. "We were a bunch of strangers before." Which is true.

DECEMBER 28

Tonight's negative statistics are (1) we lost to Atlanta and (2) Elmore Smith was 1 for 11 from the foul line. I kept telling myself, "Don't laugh. We're losing. Don't laugh." But it was hard. At one point Elmore had a three-to-make-two situation. The first one was a foot and a half short. The second one was a foot off to the right. The third one was the closest—only half a foot short. Three straight airballs from the foul line. I don't think anybody has ever done that before. Pretty soon Elmore got fouled again and some guy sitting in the front row under the basket yelled, "Don't worry. He won't make it." Even Elmore had to laugh. And he missed again.

I got in for 15 minutes—Atlanta had run away and hid by then—and missed four of the five shots I took (though with six free throws I ended up with eight points). But, ah, the one I made. I had my back to the basket when somebody threw me a pass; I had to reach over a guy's shoulder to get it. I brought the ball around underneath the basket, then flipped it up and in underhanded. I could see Chick Hearn on his feet, laughing and applauding.

But that wasn't the best thing about today for me. The best thing was that Cheryl drove down for the game. She's been home in Asheville, North Carolina, for about a week, looking after her younger brother and sister while her folks are skiing in Colorado. We had lunch before the game and a sentimental walk around Atlanta. Tonight we ordered a big room-service dinner and then, on one of those hotel television setups where you pay to watch first-run movies, we saw Charles Bronson knock off every mugger and hood in New York in *Death Wish*. We watched it twice, in fact. I wonder if there's any symbolism there.

Neither Cheryl nor I really mind my being away that much because we can look forward to being together again. I think it makes us appreciate each other more. But I don't envy the wife or girlfriend of any professional athlete. Sometimes I think they're under as much pressure as we are and have none of the rewards. It doesn't surprise me that marriages break up as much as they do in sports and that a lot of the couples who do stay together often have a rocky time. I think that may be one of the reasons Cheryl and I haven't gotten married yet. We're happy with our relationship as it is and want to let it go along like this for as long as we possibly can. I try to be aware of the problems she has that are related to the life we lead, but I know that I'm wrapped up so intensely in my own situation that it's difficult to be as sensitive to them as I ought to be. We've had a lot of long talks about this whole thing. Maybe this is a good time to let Cheryl say how she feels.

The thing that was hardest for me to get used to was Stan's identity as a public figure. I found that there are a great many subjects that I can't discuss at all—even with my best friends —because they involve his situation on the team. For instance, Susan Levin, Rich's wife, is a very good friend, but there are only certain things that I feel I can talk to her about. She loves her husband and wants to help him in his job, and if she got some little tidbit from me it would be only natural for her to pass it on to Rich. So I have to watch what I say. It would be ridiculous for me to say, "Now that's off the record, Susan." So

I just don't always confide in her the way good friends should be able to. Even people I meet casually, when they find out I'm Stan's girlfriend, will ask things like, "What do you really think of Jerry West?" And I feel I have to be guarded in what I say because I never know who is in the room and how far even my most innocuous answers will go.

Then there is the way girls come on when they're around basketball players. It's hard to look at a lot of these guys and picture them as husbands and fathers. They all project very exciting images, and to a lot of girls they are heroes. With Stan, the situation is compounded by the way he is publicly portrayed. Last year he was the only single guy on the Lakers and he's pictured as the free spirit, the ladies' man of the team, the Playboy of the Western Division with the pretty blond hair. He's tall and he stands out in any crowd, while I'm little and inconspicuous by comparison. So when we're out in public, girls will come up and whisper to him and kiss him on the ear as if I weren't even there. It takes a lot of getting used to and I haven't mastered it yet. People talk to me too, of course, but it's not the same thing. I mean, if you meet Gail and Francie Goodrich somewhere are you really interested in Francie?

I think I understand more what I'm dealing with now, but last year—the first time we had really been together—was pretty rough. Stan warned me about it, but I had always figured I could handle anything that came along and it hit me hard to realize it wasn't going to be easy.

There was just so much to get used to. To begin with, he was under terrible pressure with the Lakers. He'd come home tired and irritable from games in which he hadn't played much and I just didn't understand everything he was going through. He was far from the happiest guy in the world last season. By the end of the year he wasn't paying as much attention to me as I felt he should and I took it personally. I began to think he just didn't care. I figured, I'm not here because I love California or basketball or the good life on the beach. I am here because of him. And if he is not acting like he cares, I'm leaving.

I really needed a vacation before the season was over, but the playoffs were coming up and I felt a responsibility to stay. He thinks he can take care of himself, but he really can't. He doesn't know where his practice clothes are; he misplaces his wallet; he doesn't eat well. If I'm not around to cook he'll eat at Bob's Big Boy all the time. I seemed to be spending all my time trying to do everything I could for Stan, to take care of every detail, so he could concentrate totally on his basketball. It was no one thing that bugged me; but everything taken together, all the tension, made me mentally exhausted. I was just a zombie. But I stuck around thinking it would be only a little longer and I could hold on.

There was something else too. Stan had decided he really had to train last summer, that he had to work hard and I should go home for those months. He felt it would be very hard for him to get up every day, head out the door, and spend all his time working out if I were there. We'd just lie around all day, go on drives, and water-ski and party and have a good time. He was right, of course, but it made me mad that I had to go. I felt I had gone through the whole season, all the trouble and all the pressure, and now with the summer coming, the easy and fun time, he wants to send me home.

So finally, at the very end of the season, I took off. Stan had gone out on an errand and I just packed my stuff in my car, left a card on the refrigerator telling him I was leaving, and took off. I drove all day and got as far as Kingman, Arizona, and I called him so he wouldn't worry.

Stan was pretty mad. He said he couldn't understand why I had left like that, without even saying good-by. I had had a whole day to think about it and felt less harassed already. So the next day I turned around and came back. I stayed in Los Angeles one more day and then I started out for home the second time. I spent the summer at home in Asheville and I think it really helped us. I think people really do need to get away from each other occasionally.

DECEMBER 30

Connie Hawkins and I welcomed Kermit Washington to the doghouse tonight. The Lakers had stayed close to Houston until Kermit went in for Elmore Smith, who was having a good game, in the third quarter. Kermit's been the backup center on this trip. In fact, Zelmo Beaty hasn't played the last seven games. Kermit committed three fouls in the five minutes he played and nearly got into a fight with Steve Hawes, the Rockets' big rookie center. By the time Elmore came back in, Houston had a pretty good lead and they went on to beat us by 13 points.

It wasn't really Kermit's fault. You feel you have to be aggressive when you don't get many opportunities to play and it's easy to go overboard. You have to know you're going to have some time to settle down out there before you can relax enough not to look at every play as a life-or-death situation. But it really bugged the coaches. They think Kermit doesn't play with enough control anyhow. Kermit is very frustrated right now. Aren't we all?

The Hawk, who has started ever since the Kansas City game over a month ago, was replaced by Corky Calhoun tonight and wound up with only nine minutes of playing time, during which he didn't take one shot. After the game Rich Levin asked him what was going on and Connie, who gets along with Rich pretty well, kind of snapped at him, "Man, I don't know."

Bill Sharman explained it by saying, "Any time we play a team that runs, it's hard to use Hawkins. He kind of gets lost against a team with quickness. I never know what he's going to do." He also said he wanted Calhoun's defense against Rudy Tomjanovich. Corky played 38 minutes and Tomjanovich scored 25 points.

JANUARY 1

Last night may have been the quietest New Year's Eve I've ever spent. I got home to an empty house—Cheryl is still in Asheville—went over to Steve's for dinner, and then came home and went to bed before nine o'clock. I set the alarm for just before midnight so I could watch the Beach Boys' concert on television. Steve said their show at the Forum Friday night was a huge success. And when I got to practice today the ball boys I'd gotten tickets for were just raving about it. So were the nurses at the office of the doctor who examined this cyst that flared up on my chin a week or so ago. (He says it isn't dangerous, but if it doesn't go away they'll probably have to cut it out.)

The interesting thing about the Beach Boys is that after more than a decade of solid commercial success, they are now getting the artistic recognition they deserve. There have been some good articles about them in *Rolling Stone* and *Playboy* the last couple of months, paying tribute to their early harmonic contributions to rock and noting how the Beatles and other groups picked up on a lot of what they were doing. A great thing about their concert was that there were a tremendous number of teenagers there, a whole new generation of fans who dig them as much as the kids did when they were first starting out.

It was really cold in the Loyola gym during practice and nobody was around because it was only 10:00 A.M. New Year's Day, but we had a good workout. It was nice to have it early so I could get back to the house and have some friends over and watch some football.

JANUARY 3

When the team is going bad and you're not playing much, you get your kicks wherever you find them. Against the Celtics in the Forum tonight, for instance, we took another beating. They were up by 30 points at the end of the third quarter, and Bill Sharman cleared the bench. There was nothing to do but go out and have some fun. Which we did. We hounded the Boston reserves, put up every decent shot we had a chance at, and with a few minutes left had cut the margin down to about ten points. Not really close enough to catch them, but close enough to get them thinking about the possibility of it.

Tom Heinsohn, the Boston coach, put Dave Cowens and some of the other regulars back in and the crowd booed the shit out of him. We kind of winked at each other; it was a moral victory. There was nothing left for us to do but commit desperation fouls and we never got any closer, but it was fun to have made it a little more respectable. I scored 14 points and had six rebounds in 15 minutes, and Bill said I'd shown good movement. It was encouraging to get a good word out of him.

I'm afraid one game isn't enough, though. It's an unhappy little band of scrubeenies these days. Pat Riley's tendinitis is flaring up in his knee again and he hasn't played in the last five games. Brian Winters is very frustrated after starting out so well and then being sent to the pines. The fact that it's Stu Lantz, an experienced veteran, who has taken over as the number-three guard doesn't make it any easier on Brian. After you get a taste of jumping into the middle of things right out of college and finding out you can play this game, it's tough to settle back into a subordinate role and even sit out whole games.

And Kermit Washington is really shook. Zelmo Beaty returned to his role as Elmore Smith's backup last night after

174

missing seven straight games, and Kermit only got in for six minutes. Even the fact that he helped close the gap on the Celtics didn't put him in a very good humor. He came into the locker room and kicked all the cups and towels off a table in the middle of the room. Then he slammed his shoes into his locker and swore out loud. We're all getting bugged by the approach of the February 1 trading deadline, the possible return of Cazzie Russell in a couple of weeks, and the fact that we're not making up any ground in the division.

John Havlicek of the Celtics scored 22 points tonight and became the fifth leading scorer in NBA history, behind only Wilt Chamberlain, Oscar Robertson, Jerry West, and Elgin Baylor. Which is a pretty formidable lineup. They stopped the game and awarded him the ball. Havlicek really is an amazing player. He made some shots tonight—reverse layups and off-balance bank shots—that made me turn to the guy next to me and say, "Isn't that unbelievable?" A couple of times I felt like standing up and applauding. What an athlete he is.

JANUARY 5

An outstanding one-point overtime win over Washington, which has the best record in the league, at the Forum tonight. Gail Goodrich's ankle is bothering him again, so Stu Lantz played almost the whole game with Brian Winters, the chief backup guard. Brian won it in overtime with a desperation 30-footer with two seconds left.

The game went into overtime when Happy Hairston tied the game with just over a minute to go on the funniest three-point play I've ever seen. He scored the basket underneath, was fouled, and threw his hands up in the air and started prancing around like Muhammad Ali after knocking some-body out. Typical Happy. Then he suddenly threw one of his arms down, in the referee's signal that the basket is good, and lost his balance and fell on his back. The ultimate embarrassment. People were screaming with laughter. It was a hilarious scene, and it was a real tribute to Happy that he could make the free throw that tied the game after that.

JANUARY 7

"Two for McAdoo!" That's all we heard all night. Bob McAdoo scored 44 points and had 18 rebounds, and Buffalo beat us. We were up at the half and still in it until early in the fourth quarter, when McAdoo scored six straight points.

Bill Sharman didn't make the trip because he had to testify in Salt Lake City in a lawsuit the Utah Stars of the ABA brought against him and the Lakers. The Stars claim Bill jumped a contract when he came to the Lakers in 1971. John Barnhill is running the team. Pat Riley didn't make the trip and Connie Hawkins has an injured finger, so Brian Winters played some forward for the first time. It's another variation of the three-guard offense we ran in Baltimore. It's something Bill and John have been talking about for a while, I guess.

In the fourth quarter Happy Hairston suddenly pulled up, grabbed his knee, and came limping off the court. They put an icepack on it in the locker room. We're starting to look like a Civil War battalion again. On to Philadelphia.

JANUARY 8

During pregame warmups tonight John Barnhill called me over and told me I was starting. Happy Hairston's knee is still bothering him. I didn't have much chance to think about anything other than it's about time.

We played Philadelphia very close during the first half. It was one of those games where everybody seems to be all over everybody else and you don't see many shot opportunities. But I felt good on defense, especially at the start, and I blocked four shots, including one by Billy Cunningham on a backdoor situation. After a while I started tiring—my endurance seems down again after all the relative inactivity—and Steve Mix began beating me on the boards. Kermit Washington came in and put a stop to that immediately. It was nice to see.

We pulled away in the third period and won by eight. I ended up with eight points, and only seven shots, in 25 minutes, but Gail Goodrich had 34 points and Elmore Smith had 20. You have to play that way sometimes. If you're not getting open for shots, somebody else must be. So you keep moving the ball around, trying to find out who it is. If you're patient enough, eventually you will.

JANUARY 10

What is it with us and Boston? Twice now we have been at our lowest physical ebb when we've gotten here and by rights they should have murdered us. But we've stayed right with them, only to lose at the end. The culprit tonight was me. I plead not guilty, your honor.

Happy Hairston was back (so was Bill Sharman; they declared a mistrial), but Lucius Allen stayed at the hotel with the flu. And after playing 15 minutes, Elmore Smith had to bow out with a painful colon condition. Zelmo Beaty went the rest of the way at center (Kermit Washington never got off the bench), so we used only seven players in the second half. Even so, we were ahead by a point going into the final period; Gail Goodrich and Stu Lantz led the team with 24 points, and I had my season high of 18. In fact, Brian Winters and I scored the Lakers' first 13 points in the second quarter, and we had an eight-point lead until Boston caught us at the half 48–48.

In the fourth quarter Boston went ahead, but we cut a nine-point deficit down to two with about a minute to go. Then the Celtics committed a 24-second violation and we had the ball. Gail tried to get it in to Stu, but he was covered so Zelmo came over to help out. Just as Gail inbounded the ball, Dave Cowens pushed Zelmo—a foul the refs didn't call—and the ball tipped off his fingers and went out of bounds. Boston's ball.

The Celtics passed it around a little and suddenly I could see John Havlicek free across the court from me, in the corner. I came over from the weak side as he got the ball and moved in for a layup. I blocked the shot cleanly and the ball went out to Gail, who started to take off for the basket that would have tied the game. Then we heard the whistle.

The play took place in front of our bench and everybody came up screaming. We were all over Len Wirtz, who made the call and said my foot hit Havlicek's waist as I jumped to block the shot. If it did, I didn't feel it. Since when have they gone back to calling fouls for the most incidental kind of contact? Havlicek made the free throws and they won the game. Move over Kermit. Let me at that razor first.

JANUARY 11

First things first: John Havlicek told the Boston *Globe* it was a clean block.

Washington scored the first 13 points of the game tonight —and 15 in a row near the end. Other than that, they couldn't do a thing against us. It was the last game before the All-Star break—ten glorious days off—and our problems were all exposed for the world to see: no scoring from up front (I had ten points off the bench to lead the forwards, also nine rebounds), no consistency, no ability to capitalize on our momentum. Even after our terrible start, we caught the Bullets and actually led by a point early in the fourth quarter. But the Bullets have a lot of strength they can go to, and they just ripped off the 15 straight and put us out of our misery.

So here we are, halfway through the season, with 17 wins and 25 losses, in last place in the division, 11½ games behind the Warriors and four games out of second. Except for a guy like Gail Goodrich who will say, "Don't give up yet—keep working hard; we are still in it," our situation isn't talked about much. I think it's because the possibility that we aren't going to make the playoffs this time is becoming more real every day. Portland, Seattle, and Phoenix can't get anything going either, but it's hard to get much comfort from the fact that the reason we haven't been left behind yet by anybody but the Warriors is that the other three teams in the division are playing as badly as we are. Any one of them could get hot at any time and that would be the end of it.

I'll try to sum some of this up in a couple of days, but you'll have to excuse me now. I've got a plane to North Carolina to catch.

JANUARY 15

Eggnog and pizza for breakfast. Cheryl, please come back!

What's that old Jimmy Durante song that goes, "Sometimes I feel like I want to go and sometimes I feel like I want to stay?"

I am standing here on the second floor of my house, looking out the window through my binoculars at people playing Frisbee and football and riding bicycles. What are my thoughts? Hell, my thoughts just walked by with three footballs. They all have blond hair. How could anybody want to leave here?

But it's been almost two years and I still haven't had my shot. Will I ever? Cazzie Russell is due back at practice tomorrow, and who knows what that means? Maybe it means I'm moving on; if not now, then next season. And maybe that's the best thing. To go someplace where I can play.

I love this game too much—and the life it lets me lead—not to try to play it as long as I can, as long as I am physically productive and can earn a living. But you can't play unless people want you, and for them to want you you have to be worth something, and to be worth something you can't sit on the bench all the time. If there is no chance here, then it will have to be someplace else.

Steve says he's working on some new plans to get things off dead center. I'll be back in a couple of months to let you know how they worked out.

EPILOGUE

FEBRUARY 16

Did I say a couple of months? Make that a couple of weeks.

Dick White, our publicity man, tried to sell the press on the idea that after the All-Star break the Lakers would be starting their "second season" and making a run at second place and a playoff spot. The trouble is our second season began even worse than our first.

After all the worrying about who Cazzie Russell would replace on the roster, it turned out to be something of an anticlimax. Connie Hawkins broke a bone in a finger just before the All-Star game and it's taken a long time to heal, so he was put on the injured list and Cazzie took his spot. He gave the Lakers a little scoring punch, but he had so much trouble moving around, especially laterally, that he was probably more of a liability than a help. In his first game, for instance,

181

he scored 24 points against the Warriors, but Rick Barry scored 38—many of them while Cazzie was guarding him—and we lost by 30.

We were beaten in 8 of our first 11 games after the break (I played a total of about ten minutes in them), and if we hadn't played New Orleans twice it would have been 10 of 11. It soon became clear that the Lakers aren't going to make the playoffs for the first time since they came to Los Angeles and that decisive action was called for. So early this week they cut me.

Larry Creger called at 9:00 A.M. and said Bill Sharman wanted to see me in his office. On the way over I realized that it meant one of two things: he was going to give me another chance to play or he was going to put me on waivers. But as I walked into his office, I could tell by the look on his face that I was through as a Laker. As I listened to him, I thought about how much I had respected him at one point, how much his reputation had meant to me, and how little I thought of him now. Finally, I just couldn't help myself. I exploded.

"You lied to me," I told him. "Your judgment is all fucked up. You never gave me a chance. All that talk about statistics was just bullshit. Minute for minute, I was your top-scoring forward and your second best rebounding forward. And none of that meant anything to you, did it?"

He acted like he didn't hear me and tried to calm me down, saying he appreciated my attitude and hustle and my contributions to the team.

"Fuck it!" I shouted at him. "I don't want to hear that shit!"

"What you need is playing time," he said.

"Don't tell me that shit!" I hollered. "Here we are the worst team in the NBA—no, excuse me; New Orleans, a bullshit expansion team, is the only one worse—and I still can't play. Your judgment stinks and you're making another mistake by doing this to me."

It went on for half an hour, with him trying to calm me down while I vented my anger. I kept wishing he would throw me out. At one point I picked up the phone and said I wanted to call Steve in on our meeting because I didn't know how to deal with it.

"That's been one of your problems," he said, and he took the phone away from me.

"One of my problems, you son of a bitch, is that I don't know how to play this front-office game." I reached for the phone again, but Bill took it away again, and it's a good thing he did. I was so mad I couldn't even remember the number. In the end, when I walked out of his office, I was laughing and crying at the same time.

It didn't take me long to see that it was for the best. The injury to my pride at being rejected and the anger at the unfairness of not getting a real chance are what made me blow up. But when I had time to think about the situation as unemotionally as possible and to talk about it with my friends, I realized again—as I had months earlier—that I had to get away from the Lakers. Less than an hour after I left Bill's office, in fact, people were kidding me about it and I was trying to recover my sense of humor.

"I've got a nine-to-four job open," said my friend Alan, who owns a gas station.

"I've got a truckdriver's position you can have," offered my good friend Tom.

As soon as I got in touch with Steve after leaving Bill's office, he got on the phone. The San Antonio Spurs of the ABA —they're the old Dallas franchise that drafted me out of college—told him they were eager to have me. Steve said we shouldn't be in any hurry, that we should check out any other possibilities. But the Spurs insisted we fly down this weekend, and when we got there they made us an offer we couldn't refuse. We came back to LA tonight, and had a celebration dinner with our girlfriends. In two days Cheryl and I will fly to San Antonio.

Today I got to thinking about something that happened in Buffalo during our last road trip. I was sitting on the end of the bench looking at about 20 kids in wheelchairs, kids who were destroyed physically, and I thought about growing up and going through college and making it to the pros. As I looked at those kids, I thought, How bad can it be? It's been a nice two years—living at home, being with my family and friends—and now it's time to move on.

While I was remembering those thoughts, the phone rang. It was Brian Winters. "Somebody wants to talk to you," he said.

"He got you fired, man," a voice yelled over the phone. I could hear Brian giggling in the background. "He started playing forward and he got you fired."

"Shit, Hawk," I hollered back, tears of laughter streaming down my face, "you got me fired."

I'm going to miss you, Hawk, I thought as I put the phone down. All you guys, in fact. But for now would you mind stepping back a bit and getting out of the way? Move over some, fellows. Here comes Love in the ABA.

B

LOV

76- 2401

Love, Stan

Love in the NBA

DATE DUE

28 '7 3-76			